W9-DAM-736

# THE ROMAN FORUM

WONDERS OF THE WORLD

..............................

# THE ROMAN FORUM

## DAVID WATKIN

Harvard University Press
Cambridge, Massachusetts
2009

Printed in the United States of America

First published in the United Kingdom by
Profile Books, Ltd.
3A Exmouth House
Pine Street
London EC1R OJH

Library of Congress Cataloging-in-Publication Data

Watkin, David, 1941-
The Roman Forum / David Watkin.
p. cm.
First published: London : Profile Books, 2009.
Includes bibliographical references and index.
ISBN 978-0-674-03341-2 (alk. paper)
1. Roman Forum (Rome, Italy) 2. Historic buildings—Italy—Rome.
3. Rome (Italy)—Buildings, structures, etc. 4. Architecture, Roman—Italy—
Rome. 5. Piranesi, Giovanni Battista, 1720–1778. 6. Rome (Italy)—Antiquities.
7. City and town life—Italy—Rome—History. 8. Rome (Italy)—Social life and
customs. 9. Rome—Antiquities. 10. Rome—Social life and customs.
I. Title.
DG66.5.W38 2009
954′.632—dc22
2009006785

# CONTENTS

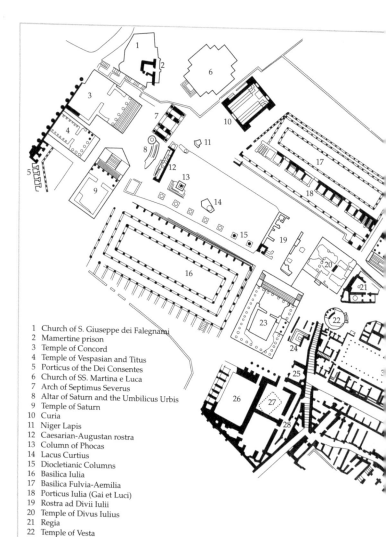

1 Church of S. Giuseppe dei Falegnami
2 Mamertine prison
3 Temple of Concord
4 Temple of Vespasian and Titus
5 Porticus of the Dei Consentes
6 Church of SS. Martina e Luca
7 Arch of Septimus Severus
8 Altar of Saturn and the Umbilicus Urbis
9 Temple of Saturn
10 Curia
11 Niger Lapis
12 Caesarian-Augustan rostra
13 Column of Phocas
14 Lacus Curtius
15 Diocletianic Columns
16 Basilica Iulia
17 Basilica Fulvia-Aemilia
18 Porticus Iulia (Gai et Luci)
19 Rostra ad Divii Iulii
20 Temple of Divus Iulius
21 Regia
22 Temple of Vesta
23 Temple of Castor and Pollux
24 Fountain of Juturna
25 Oratory of the Forty Martyrs
26 Domitianic Hall
27 Church of S. Maria Antiqua
28 Covered ramp to Palatine

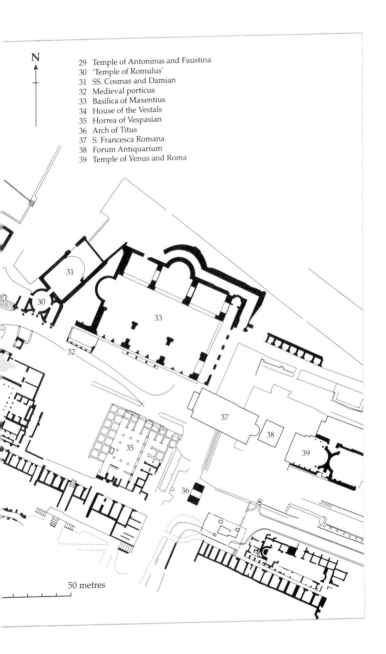

N

29 Temple of Antoninus and Faustina
30 'Temple of Romulus'
31 SS. Cosmas and Damian
32 Medieval porticus
33 Basilica of Maxentius
34 House of the Vestals
35 Horrea of Vespasian
36 Arch of Titus
37 S. Francesca Romana
38 Forum Antiquarium
39 Temple of Venus and Roma

50 metres

# NOTE ON THE TEXT

Though the axis of the Forum from the Tabularium to the Arch of Titus is not strictly west–east, it is sufficiently close to enable the terms north, south, east and west to be used in this book, rather than north-east, north-west, etc.

# INTRODUCTION

The Roman Forum is one of the most famous of all historic sites, the heart of the ancient city, the hub of the Roman empire, the goal of tens of thousands of Grand Tourists. It is still visited by millions of people a year, yet it can be a baffling experience. Partly this is because archaeologists dig deeper and deeper in the understandable pursuit of knowledge about Rome and its early history, leaving behind rubble and holes which are ugly and difficult to understand. It is also because some of the most prominent monuments, which are believed by almost all visitors to be antique, turn out essentially to be products of the nineteenth or twentieth century.

The period when it was in use by the ancient Romans as a working Forum was far shorter than the millennium and a half that has passed since the fall of their Empire, during which time it has inspired countless artists and architects. However, archaeologists have eliminated much evidence of the fascinating post-antique life of the Forum, including the contributions to it of architects and planners from the sixteenth century onwards. Some of the churches that both replaced and yet continued the life of the temples and shrines of the ancient Forum have been demolished, often with no proper record made. A wiser approach now prevails elsewhere, as in the current conservation of the town of Butrint in Albania, which retains evidence of prehistoric occupation and of its role as a Greek colony, a Roman city and a bishopric, with elements deriving from Byzantine rule, Venetian occupation and from the late Middle Ages. All of these are now being preserved as equal parts of a rich narrative, following the designation of the place as a World Heritage Site in 1993.

The end of archaeology's domination of the Forum is long overdue. This book sets out to encourage exactly that by taking a totally new look at it, attempting to show it once more as a genial and humane place to visit, comprehensible yet full of resonance, 'that lovely lake of time', as Eleanor Clark described it in 1976. The most vivid and instructive visual record of the Forum are the eighteenth century engravings of Giovanni Battista Piranesi, the greatest engraver of all time. He has been a helpful guide in the writing of this book on the Forum, for he recorded it at the last time when it was still a place of poetry, capable of inspiring great painters, writers and thinkers, like Claude, Gibbon and Goethe. Its ancient ruins were then in suggestive contrast to signs of modern life and human habitation: its churches opened into it, not on to outside roads, it featured a gushing water trough and also a generous avenue of elm trees laid out as part of the Baroque replanning of Rome in the seventeenth century under the great builder pope, Alexander VII.

'There is no more historic place than the Roman Forum,' according to the authoritative *Rome: An Oxford Archaeological Guide* (1998). After all, it was the juridical, administrative and commercial centre of Republican Rome and later became the key symbol of Roman imperial power. It was the place where Julius Caesar's corpse was cremated, where Cicero's oratory

1. *View from window in the Palazzo Senatorio (Piranesi,* Vedute di Roma, c. *1748–78).* The Arch of Septimius Severus and Temple of Vespasian, both partly buried, are in the foreground with behind them the Column of Phocas, flanked by houses. The dull pedimented façade of the Senate House on the left-hand side is linked to a long line of houses leading to the Temple of Antoninus and Faustina.

[ 3 ]

found full expression, but where, after his execution, his head and hands were nailed to the Rostra on Mark Antony's orders. Yet, despite the emphasis of *Rome: An Oxford Archaeological Guide* on the Forum as 'historic', the illustration on its front cover is of the Temple of Vesta, built in 1930 under Mussolini, and it is not identified as 'modern' in the caption. It is one of the aims of this book to uncover such paradoxes, which, properly understood, are one of the riches of the Forum yet are often overlooked by visitors who come expecting to see exclusively 'ancient' Roman monuments.

We must accept what the guidebooks cannot say: that much of what we see is not ancient and that many of the ruins can be baffling, ugly and frustrating, their original function remaining obscure, despite the confident claims of archaeologists. The novelist James Joyce, shocked as early as 1906 by the impact of mass tourism, wrote ironically to his brother, 'I must be a very insensible person. Yesterday I went to see the Forum. I sat down on a stone bench overlooking the ruins … Carriages full of tourists, postcard sellers, medal sellers, photograph sellers. I was so moved that I almost fell asleep … So I went home sadly. Rome reminds me of a man who lives by exhibiting to travellers his grandmother's corpse.' As H. V. Morton complained in 1957, 'The visitors peering about the ruins with maps remind one of people looking for a buried safe.' It has been recently claimed that, even as early as the fifteenth and sixteenth centuries, 'Renaissance men, living in its ruins, were right to be amazed: it must have felt like living in New York, a century after the explosion of a neutron bomb.'

Archaeologists are even now daily unearthing fragmentary foundations of long-vanished ancient Roman buildings at many levels, representing different periods of time. Though instructive to scholars, these are more or less impenetrable to everyone else and make visiting parts of the Forum about as attractive as looking into the hole made in New York on 9/11. One easy method of making a more cheerful visit is to explore on the Roman Forum website the model of it made by Robert Garbisch in 1982, at Brandeis University in Massachusetts, which shows it 'on a summer's day on the last visit of Marcus Aurelius in AD 179'. We can travel through a series of thirty-five views which, though often conjectural and somewhat coarse in detail, give a vivid impression of life in the ancient Forum.

Visitors to the Forum will assume from what they have read about it that it is the one place where they can most readily see ancient Roman monuments. However, much of what we see of any magnitude, except for the Tabularium (originally the record office of Rome), the Arch of Septimius Severus (commemorating that emperor's victories in the East), the three columns of the temples of Vespasian and of Castor and Pollux, and the fragments of the Basilica of Maxentius, dates from the Early Christian period and the Middle Ages, the Renaissance and Baroque periods, and the nineteenth and twentieth centuries. There are also frequent reconstructions and rebuilds, often unrecognised by the modern visitor. For example, the Portico of the Harmonious Gods, the Temple of Vesta and the Shrine of Juturna date respectively from the 1850s, 1930s and 1950s. The Temple of Antoninus and Faustina has become the Renaissance church of S. Lorenzo in Miranda; much of the Arch of Titus, save for its sculptural decoration, is nineteenth century; the Rostra is of 1904; and the Curia, or Senate House, as well as the more meagre remains of the Temple of Divus Julius, also owe much to twentieth-century rebuilding.

Archaeologists from the early nineteenth century on began to believe that post-antique buildings in the Forum are of little or no interest. A typical fruit of this is the astonishing claim in 1882 by the leading archaeologist Rodolfo Lanciani that the sixteenth- and seventeenth-century Farnese Gardens and pavilions on the edge of the Forum 'were born with a heavy original sin – that of concealing, of disfiguring, and of cutting piecemeal the magnificent ruins of the imperial palace'. His religious hatred of the remains of these beautiful gardens and buildings, carefully aligned on the Basilica of Maxentius, blinded him to the fact that the 'magnificent ruins' were mainly little more than foundations.

To discover that chronology in the Forum is not always what it seems does not diminish its interest – rather the reverse in my view – but it makes its significance somewhat different from what is generally supposed. There are also a handful of buildings whose functions we do not know, and others which are not normally visited or described in guidebooks, which tend to have a selective vision, often failing even to mention some of the most significant monuments. To visit the Forum is to be told a story of what, during the last millennium and a half, people have thought it should look like rather than what it did look like. The trouble is that this is not made clear in the guidebooks to it, in the histories of it, or in the ways in which it is shown to visitors.

One should go to this historic site expecting not only to see the ancient Roman Forum but also to enjoy the visible complexities of use and re-use and the resonances of the rich narrative unfolded within it. This includes four churches which incorporate ancient Roman buildings: S. Lorenzo in Miranda, built inside the Temple of Antoninus and Faustina but open for only two hours a week; SS. Cosmas and Damian, formed out of an audience hall in the Temple of Peace of the fourth century AD; S. Maria Antiqua, an adaptation in the mid or late sixth century of a peristyle atrium and forecourt of the late first century, not always open to the public; and S. Giuseppe dei Falegnami (St Joseph of the Carpenters), begun at the end of the sixteenth century over the ancient Roman Mamertine Prison.

This book will thus explain places and buildings in the Forum which many guidebooks do not mention and do not want us to see, because they regard the place as essentially an archaeological site to be visited solely for evidence of ancient Roman buildings. It is hoped that we shall find the Forum a much fuller and more exciting place than this, discovering, for example, that the whole place has been turned inside out. This is because the churches of S. Lorenzo in Miranda, SS. Cosmas and Damian and S. Francesca Romana, though all incorporating antique Roman elements and once integral parts of the open space of the Forum, have each turned their backs on it and can no longer be entered from it.

To demonstrate our point further, let us look at one key building, the Temple of Antoninus and Faustina (see fig. 2). Begun in AD 140 by the Emperor Antoninus Pius in memory of his wife, Faustina, it was rebuilt as the church of S. Lorenzo in Miranda, possibly in the seventh or eighth century, though it first appears in documents in 1074. It was completely rebuilt in the seventeenth century. Guidebooks always describe it as a Roman temple, largely ignoring the charm provided by its layered character, which makes it the equivalent of a manuscript where one piece of writing has been overlaid or effaced by a later hand. Inside the church,

2. *Temple of Antoninus and Faustina (Piranesi,* Vedute di Roma, c. *1748–78).*
Inside the ancient Roman temple is the Baroque church of S. Lorenzo in
Miranda. Excavation of the floor of the Forum down to the ancient Roman
level has meant that the entrance door seen here is now stranded about half
way up the façade.

the floor on which one stands was inserted into the building in the seventeenth century when the bottom of the Forum was filled up to that great height with earth and rubble. Since excavations from the early nineteenth century have removed that infill, the doors of the church, when viewed from the Forum, are now stranded half way up its façade. There is no clearer place than this to grasp the complicated history of the layers of the Forum.

One of the most breathtaking experiences one can have here is to be present inside this temple-cum-church when the ancient doors at the end of the nave, normally kept locked, are opened to reveal a unique panoramic view of the Forum through the giant columns of the temple. It is greatly to be regretted that such an intensely evocative experience, in which the religions of the pagan and Christian world coincide, is little experienced by the public since the building is so rarely open. It thus plays no part in the image of the Forum carried away by most visitors, though it is fortunate that its Baroque façade behind the Roman columns has not yet been destroyed in the supposed interests of archaeology. Moreover, as well as its pagan and Christian associations, the church has acquired another and unexpected use as the seat of a chemical and pharmaceutical college, which has arranged a stylish museum in the lower church for the display of historic objects such as pestles, mortars and painted jugs, from pharmacies and chemists' shops. The changing functions of ancient buildings is, of course, a feature of Rome that makes the entire city fascinating to visit.

Nonetheless, much of the Forum is now dominated by bits of rubble, holes that might have been filled by posts in the eighth century BC, and metal barriers guarding virtually

[ 9 ]

incomprehensible foundations and puzzling scraps of often minor buildings of uncertain function. Yet, when rightly approached, the Forum is a magical place. It is hoped that this book will make this clear and will be enjoyed by readers at home as well as serving as a guide when they visit it. Having explained the role of the Forum in the ancient world in the first chapter, we shall begin to explore it in the present day with Piranesi as our guide.

# I

................................................................

# LIFE IN THE FORUM IN ANTIQUITY

The setting of some of the most illustrious – and murderous – events in the history of the world, the Roman Forum evokes the names of great leaders of men, from the mythical Romulus, through Augustus, to Constantine. Yet this original paved area from the imperial Rostra in the north to the Temple of Divus Julius in the south was no bigger than a football pitch and was architecturally a muddle of buildings, arches and statues, jammed against each other without symmetry or visual coherence. It was here that the body of the dictator Julius Caesar, assassinated in the name of liberty, was cremated in 44 BC; here that Mark Antony harangued his 'friends, Romans, countrymen'; here that Cicero railed against the conspiracy of Catiline in speeches that have been studied, admired and deplored ever since; and here in 69 AD that the elderly emperor Galba was knocked out of his litter and decapitated.

For the ancient Romans, the Forum was many things: market, exchange, tribunal, open-air public meeting hall, and setting for the sacrifices to the gods on which the stability of the state was believed to depend. The triumphal processions of victorious emperors and generals passed through it on an east-to-west route on their way up to the Capitoline

3. *Virtual reconstruction of the Forum, looking east.* The Basilica Aemilia on the
left-hand-side faces the Basilica Julia across the open space at the far end of
which is the Temple of Divus Julius with behind it the House of the Vestal
Virgins. The prominent row of honorific columns was added when the
Basilica Julia was built in its final form by Diocletian after the fire of AD 283.

Hill above (we should remember that the Forum was always a public thoroughfare). Vitruvius, author in the first century BC of *Ten Books on Architecture*, the only surviving ancient treatise on its subject, explained that a forum should contain money-changers' shops and that basilicas, a treasury, a prison and a senate house should adjoin it. Though we now think of the Roman Forum largely in terms of public and political life, it was a town centre that was home to figures ranging from flower-sellers and jewellers to prostitutes, and it was alive with private houses as late as the second century BC. Moreover, long before the building of the nearby Colosseum from AD 75 to 80, it was the setting for gladiatorial shows and wild beast hunts; in fact, a system of underground tunnels through which the beasts might be let out into the open space of the Forum has been excavated.

It is with religion, however, that we should begin: indeed, temples to the gods form the majority of the ancient structures still standing or reconstructed in the Forum. Though sacred buildings were found in many other places in Rome – so many that the emperor Augustus could plausibly claim to have restored eighty-two of them – the Forum was perhaps the main focus of the religious activity of Rome. By the age of Julius Caesar, it already contained four historic temples – Saturn, Concord, Vesta, and Castor and Pollux – and twice as many by the end of the third century AD, with temples of Vespasian, Antoninus and Faustina, Venus Genetrix, and Venus and Roma added, omitting the early fourth-century 'Divus Romulus'.

In their form, siting and ornament, temples played a central role in Roman religious experience. Yet, as with Greek temples, the primary role of the Roman temple was to house

[ 13 ]

an awesome image of the deity, not to provide a welcoming space for a congregation. Ritual and sacrifice took place in front of the temple: following the sacrifice of the animal its organs were removed, and if they were found to be in perfect condition they were taken as a good omen. The Forum was used for communal feasting in a quasi-religious context, Livy noting a funeral feast in 183 BC there when it was so windy that diners had to set up little tents as wind breaks round their tables. Ironically, the pagan practice of performing rituals in the open air has recently been re-adopted in Rome where the pope, the Pontifex Maximus (chief priest), a title borrowed from pagan Rome and adopted by the papacy in the fifteenth century, conducts the Sacrifice of the Mass out of doors on important occasions against the backdrop of the entrance façade of St Peter's Basilica (which, it has been said, has become the most under-used church in Christendom).

In ancient Rome, the sacrificial animal was divided into parts, some of which, possibly the less palatable, were cut into a number of manageable lumps and burnt as offerings to the gods, the remaining parts being consumed in a hall or tent near the temple at what were great communal occasions. The ancient Roman Forum was thus a space of religious killing and, almost certainly, communal eating.

The function of temples was not only what we could call 'religious', for though they did not hold the equivalent of a modern congregation, their interiors were far from redundant. They served a variety of religious and secular functions such as treasuries and museums, while their porticoes and steps were used as platforms for political meetings. The Temple of Castor and Pollux, for example, one of the most ancient temples of the Forum, dating back to the fifth century BC, had a giant podium from which orators addressed the crowds, while inside the podium were vaults serving as safe-deposits for private citizens and as a public treasury. Fittings housed inside the temple itself included a set of standard weights and measures and a copy, on a bronze tablet, of a fourth-century law.

Underlying these diverse uses is the Roman assumption that politics and religion were closely bound up, almost identical spheres of operation. This is why the Senate, the main Roman council of ex-magistrates, always met in a religious space. It often convened in temples in the Forum like that of Castor and Pollux. But the Senate House itself, though not a temple in the modern sense, was a *templum*, a space with a special relationship to the gods. More than this, the passing of laws and the holding of elections, as well as meetings of the assemblies, all also took place at sites which, like those of the temples, were chosen for ritual reasons by the Roman priests, known as the augurs. To help them in this process they interpreted the will of the gods through the observation of natural events such as the flight of birds, or thunder and lightning.

The Forum was, then, a sacred as well as a public, political and commercial place. Unlike Christians, who more often chose to venerate saints and martyrs, Romans based their myths on places. The sacral nature of the site of the Forum was part of a major axiom of Roman life, which said that if the Roman citizens properly honoured the gods, the gods in turn would protect the Roman state. This meant that it would be improvident for citizens to allow temples to fall into decay. As the poet Horace put it in his *Odes* in 28–27 BC, 'You will continue to pay for the sins of your fathers, Roman, though innocent yourself, until you restore the crumbling temples and shrines of the gods and their statues filthy with black smoke.'

Throughout Roman history, the link between religion and power was demonstrated by political leaders and emperors who founded temples to emphasise their authority. The Roman Forum was the key site of this symbolic display. Such buildings might be financed from the fruits of military campaigns and be thank-offerings to the gods as well as memorialising Roman history and adding to the current prestige of Rome. Politicians were expected to respect the memory of the foundation of the Roman state, so that those who commissioned buildings similarly recalled the key monuments of the early Republic: the Temple of Castor and Pollux, for example, was thrice rebuilt.

## ORIGINS

Roman mythology was everywhere coloured by the sites and monuments of Rome itself. This was encapsulated in the *Aeneid*, the epic poem by Virgil, written in 30–19 BC at just the time that, following the death of Caesar, the so-called 'free' republic was being replaced by the one-man rule of the Empire. In fact, Virgil is said to have read parts of the *Aeneid* to the first Emperor, Augustus, in 23 BC. According to Virgil, Aeneas escapes from the Trojan Wars at the fall of Troy in the twelfth century BC, and travels to Italy, where he becomes the originator of the future Roman state. The appearance of Aeneas in Homer's *Iliad*, if only in a supporting role, had already given Rome a respectable Greek ancestry.

On his arrival in Rome, Aeneas finds it already occupied as a settlement under King Evander, who, according to myth, had brought his fellow countrymen from Arcadia in central Greece to the banks of the Tiber, and there founded a colony at a place where Rome later stood. He built a city, Pallanteum, on the Palatine Hill. Evander takes Aeneas on an imaginary journey, explaining the origin and meaning of many of the future sites and names of the city down the centuries. They visit the Tarpeian Rock, the Capitol, and Evander's palace on the Palatine Hill, which rises from the south side of the future Forum. Virgil enjoys telling us that the only sound that could be heard coming from the Forum at this remote time was the lowing of cattle. This was in contrast with the busy life of the Forum in his day but, ironically, he could not have realised that by the time of Piranesi in the eighteenth century, the Forum would once again become nothing more than a Field of Cows (the 'Campo Vaccino', as it was then called).

Evander is not usually thought of as the founder of Rome, a title to which Aeneas has a claim. It is true that evidence has been found of settlements near the Tiber from about 1500 BC and, half a century later in the Iron Age, of a cemetery on the site of the Forum, which was then a swampy marsh. But according to ancient and enduring tradition, Romulus and Remus, descendants of Aeneas and twin children of Mars, founded Rome in the mid eighth century BC. In a myth which served to emphasise the religious foundation of Roman political power, an omen in the form of a flight of wild birds determined that Romulus rather than Remus should be king, and so he gave his name to the new foundation. Almost certainly this is pure myth, but archaeologists continue over-optimistically to seek evidence of historical fact embedded in the story. The excavation in the 1980s by Professor Andrea Carandini of the foundations of a substantial wall, dated to the eighth century BC, on the edge of the Forum at the foot of the Palatine was hailed as confirmation of the building of a wall by Romulus to define the *pomerium*, the sacred boundary of the city. In 2005 Carandini excavated what he considered to be a series of interesting holes in the Forum, near the Temple of Antoninus and Faustina, boldly claiming that the wooden posts of the palace of Romulus had been inserted into them.

The mythical history of early Rome was transmuted into fact by numerous authors, notably Livy in his celebrated history of Rome, begun in *c.* 27 BC. In this narrative, Romulus is said to have been succeeded by six kings, of whom the last three were Etruscans from the region west and north of Rome. Etruscans have a romantic and slightly mysterious reputation in the modern world, at least in part derived from D. H. Lawrence's posthumous book of essays *Etruscan Places* (1932). Archaeology shows them to have had a mastery of stone construction, as we can see in their fine rock-cut tombs, often with rich coloured decoration and stucco work, for example at Perugia, Tarquinia and Chiusi. They were also credited in Roman literature with all kinds of engineering and new construction in Rome, including the foundation of the great Temple of Jupiter Optimus Maximus on the Capitoline Hill. Exactly what kind of political takeover of early Rome by outsiders this represents remains a matter of debate, but the 'Etruscan' period was crucial for the development of the Forum. Naturally swampy ground, it was drained for the first time through what the Romans later knew as the Cloaca Maxima (the Great Drain). The Etruscans were also able to pave the area, which established the Forum as a civic as well as a residential centre, with buildings for religious, political and commercial functions visited by merchants, craftsmen, farmers and shepherds.

The story is that the last of the Etruscan kings, Tarquinius Superbus, was ejected as an alien tyrant by the Romans in 510 BC when they established the Republic, a fiercely anti-monarchical form of government. Its complicated constitution was never written down, though it was based on numerous laws dividing the governing bodies into what we would call executive, legislative and judicial branches in a way that has sometimes been seen as a model for the American system. The fact that the American Congress still meets on the 'Capitol' is a reflection of this influence. In the Republic, the office of king was replaced by the popular election of two consuls, serving as chief magistrates for a year at a time, drawn from the aristocratic class. Other officials were also drawn from the aristocracy, but these were subject to popular election. Together these people made up the Senate, a permanent council of between 300 and 900 members, composed largely of magistrates and ex-magistrates.

It is hard to describe this form of government. On the surface, it resembles rule by wealthy landed aristocrats, but in fact these aristocrats could not rely on simply inheriting political power: they had to stand in competition with one another for election by the people. Responding to this apparent contradiction, Polybius, the Greek historian of the second century BC, described the constitution as 'mixed', comprising oligarchic, monarchical and democratic elements, which he identified respectively with the Senate, the annually elected magistrates, and the popular assemblies or tribunes comprised magistrates elected by the people to represent their own interests.

The fundamental characteristic of political life under the *res publica* was the public demonstration of political power on the stages provided by the city of Rome: its buildings, urban spaces and, most importantly, the Forum. This power was communicated through the idiosyncratic rituals of the Republican constitution, which puzzle us as much as they did Polybius. However, this broadly democratic and competitive constitution, though frequently disrupted and challenged, lasted until the civil wars in the first century and the dictatorship of Julius Caesar.

The Forum was established from the start as the political and symbolic centre of this Republican city state, which grew to be the capital of Italy by the third century BC, dominating the Mediterranean world through warfare and conquest during the next century. The Forum was a public space for a range of activities including political meetings, riots, gladiatorial combats and funerals. Polybius wrote that, 'Whenever any famous man dies in Rome, he is carried at his funeral into the Forum with every kind of honour to the so-called Rostra,' the speaking platform from where a discourse on his virtues would be given. Near to markets, the Forum also contained food stalls and was surrounded by aristocratic houses, but increasingly it came to acquire major public buildings: the Tabularium, thought to have been a record office, and three temples, one dedicated to Saturn, sometimes seen as a god of sowing or seed-corn, one to Castor and Pollux, twin gods and semi-mythical cavalry heroes, and one to Concord, the latter built by a consul in 121 BC to commemorate a victory of the aristocracy over democracy. From the second century BC a new building type, the basilica, also appeared in the Forum: the Basilica Sempronia (169 BC) and the Basilica Paulli (55

BC) lined the south and north sides of the Forum respectively. Thus, from a paved market and assembly space, the Forum was transformed into a dignified civic and religious centre during the Republic.

## THE ROLE AND LEGACY OF CAESAR AND AUGUSTUS

We tend to think of the Forum in its Republican guise, partly because of its association with famous names like Sulla and Cicero, but its appearance was completely transformed by Julius Caesar (100–44 BC) and by his great-nephew, Octavian (63 BC–AD 14), whom he adopted as his heir. Octavian became the first emperor in 27 BC, when he was given the honorific title of Augustus ('reverend') – a nice coinage that managed to sound dignified while avoiding monarchical associations, although, in fact, it was he who brought in one-man rule following the assassination of Caesar. Though civil wars in the first century BC had slowed down building in the Forum, Caesar set about its total replanning. When he became Pontifex Maximus in 63 BC, he took up residence in the Forum in the chief priest's official residence, the Domus Publica ('public house') on its southern edge. He subsequently did much to emphasise the west–east axis of the Forum by rebuilding, as we shall see, the Rostra at the western end of this axis, and by building the Basilica Julia, principally consisting of law courts, along its south side to replace, in much more impressive style, the Basilica Sempronia.

In 54 BC, Caesar began to construct a new forum named after himself, immediately to the north of the old Roman Forum. This was the start of a now confusing range of new fora, which from this point on took over some of the functions of the old civic centre – though they never rivalled it in symbolic power. Dio Cassius, writing his *Roman History* in the early third century, claimed that around the end of the first century Caesar's Forum was 'distinctly more beautiful than the Roman Forum; yet it had increased the reputation of the other so that it was called the Great Forum'. Providing more space for the activities of the Roman Forum, especially the law courts, it was a carefully planned space on a Greek model unlike the old Forum, which – even if repeatedly tidied up – had developed piecemeal over the centuries. Its axis was dominated by the Temple of Venus, which honoured this goddess as a universal mother from whom the family of Julius Caesar claimed descent. It was Caesar who began in Rome the cult of the ruler hero, hailed as almost a god: in fact, after his assassination and cremation in the Forum, he was officially declared divine.

Augustus, a man of learning and taste, became the most important figure in the development of the Forum when he took up Caesar's move towards stressing its civic identity and dignity. In this process, he found a convenient tool in the patriotic history of Rome written by his friend Livy, while in commissioning public buildings as a way of enhancing his authority he followed the recommendation of Vitruvius, who dedicated his treatise on architecture to him. A novel element of the projects of Augustus was his use of huge quantities of marble from the quarries at Carrara (ancient Luni) in Tuscany. Marble had been much less used as a building material in the Republican period, when it was normally imported from Greece. Most buildings in the Forum at that time were of tufa, a rough porous stone, brown in colour, or of travertine, a textured cream limestone from the Tiber Valley near Rome – both materials being generally covered with stucco. It is only during the reign of Augustus that the Forum begins to take on the appearance familiar to us from modern re-creations of the city, as he replaced the provincial building materials with gleaming white marble. This was a luxury stone previously more common in the villas of aristocrats, though it had been used before when coloured Greek marbles featured in temporary theatres put up in the city.

As first emperor, Augustus made sure through his building programme that Rome was the right place for him to rule from. It was a time of religious reform in which he revived ancient priesthoods, restoring distant cults and reinstating their rituals, dress and chants. He was named Pontifex Maximus in 12 BC and deified after his death, like Julius Caesar. His claim to have built or restored eighty-two temples in a single year was surely exaggerated, but he certainly restored the temples of Saturn, Castor and Pollux, and Concord, all in the Forum, as well as erecting civic buildings and arches and forming streets. Indeed, the Forum must have been a near-intolerable building site throughout his reign. One of his most significant alterations here was to define its shape by building the Temple of Divus Julius on open land at the centre of its east end. Commemorating the cremation on this spot of the now deified Julius Caesar, this temple also brought an axial symmetry to the whole area, blocking off its east end, matching the Rostra to the west. No less importantly, it established a precedent for subsequent emperors to build monuments celebrating the cult of divine emperors, thus completely altering the character and role of the Republican Forum, previously defined by its temples to the mysterious god Saturn (the Greek Cronos), and to the twin gods, Castor and Pollux, heroic young cavalrymen.

Nonetheless, the Forum in the imperial age retained the general pattern laid out in the Republic, although many of its monuments were now sumptuously rebuilt and temples of imperial gods added, notably of Antoninus and Faustina and of Vespasian. The two long sides of its open rectangular space, although not exactly parallel to each other, were marked on the south by Caesar's Basilica Julia and on the north by the Basilica Aemilia, and the Senate House was given its final form in a rebuild by Diocletian in the third century AD. Near this, towards the west end of the Forum was the Rostra, while further west the Republican Tabularium closed the Forum at that end. As we have noted, the addition by Augustus of the Temple to Divus Julius marks the eastern end of the Forum. However, though the area thus outlined defines what we might call the Forum proper, the area to the east of it, right up to and including the Arch of Titus on the Sacred Way, also normally counts as part of the Forum. Indeed, it contains key monuments such as the Temple of Vesta and the House of the Vestals as well as the Basilica of Maxentius.

In addition to giving the Forum its most familiar shape, Augustus like Caesar built on its north side a new Forum, of which a prime purpose was to emphasise his power and authority, though Suetonius claimed that it was built because the two existing fora had become inadequate to deal with the law-suits required by the increasing population of Rome (by this point roughly a million people). At the head of the Forum of Augustus was the Temple of Mars Ultor (the war-god Mars the Avenger), used for occasional meetings of the Senate, despite the diminished role of this Republican body under the Empire. Indeed, monumental buildings often do not mark, as they appear to, the apogee of the power structure for which they were erected, but its end. The Saepta Julia near the Pantheon were built as voting halls in 26 BC at the moment when the Empire was about to end popular votes. Instead, they were mostly used for gladiatorial displays. Similarly, Lutyens' vast Viceroy's House in New Delhi was opened in 1931, just sixteen years before the extinction of the Indian Empire.

Though the old Forum was already a symbol of imperial power by the time of the funeral rites of Augustus in AD 14, it was probably less impressive than either the Forum of Augustus or the Campus Martius, which became a centre for architectural display and experimentation. Indeed, when the Greek writer Strabo (*c.* 64 BC–AD 19) gave a full account of Rome in his long treatise on geography, he scarcely mentioned the old Forum. He merely wrote: 'or you might go through the old agora [forum] and see other agorai [forums] arranged one after another with basilicas and temples'.

Nonetheless, the example of Augustus as a builder was followed by successive emperors, so that the Forum became an ever more crowded historical monument or museum. Eventually, it was 'as though there were fifteen Westminster Abbeys each within a few yards of the next', as Michael Grant put it in *The Roman Forum* (1970). Augustus was the last to allow wild-beast hunts in the Forum, for they were soon transferred elsewhere, along with the gladiatorial shows that had been a feature of life in the Forum. The narrow spaces of the Forum were no longer crowded with live animals; rather, statues and marble effigies of dead emperors and generals jostled for attention along the eight roads that threaded their way round the Forum, from the oldest, the tortuous Via Sacra (Sacred Way), to the absurdly narrow Vicus Tuscus (Tuscan Street), only thirteen and a half feet wide. Through these crowded

4. *Part of a scale model of Rome in the time of Constantine, made in 1937 (Museo della Civiltà Romana, Rome)*. In this section of the vast model we are looking north over the Forum. Near the middle on the south side is the Temple of Castor and Pollux and almost opposite this the Temple of Antoninus and Faustina from which in a row running east are the 'Temple of Romulus', Basilica of Maxentius, and the enormous Temple of Venus and Roma, close to the Colosseum.

spaces passed, as we have noted, the triumphal processions that the Senate granted to victorious generals.

The Forum Romanum remained throughout the imperial period what it had become by the end of the Republic: the centre of the world to which citizens of the vast Roman Empire were constantly drawn and in which their representatives were anxious to erect inscriptions recording their official roles. It is an indication of the importance to the ancient Romans of custom and settled ideas that power should have remained centred on the city of Rome, even though the Senate had become something of a shadow. Rome is often described today as having been purely a 'consumer city', but this, as Robert Coates-Stephens observes,

> *overlooks its role as a vast producer of luxury goods, book rolls, statues, art and architecture, including the brick, terra cotta, and pottery industries. It was also a centre for education in all of the arts, the law, administration and bureaucracy, the products of which were then exported throughout the empire along with their related personnel. And this is to ignore the tremendous achievement in literature!*

In the late first and early second centuries AD, the Emperors Domitian and Trajan followed the example of Caesar and Augustus in relieving congestion in the Forum by building yet more new fora on its north side. Though symmetrical, colonnaded spaces with a formal magnificence, these lacked the ancient historical resonances and magic of the crowded Roman Forum, which was thus never a dead place. However, exactly how the old and new fora related to each other is made almost impossible to assess by later interventions on the site: in particular Mussolini's great road, the Via de Impero (now the Via dei Fori Imperiali), which has obliterated much of their plans and the link between them and the Roman Forum.

As a balance to the possibly rather too grave picture we have painted of the Forum with its gods and heroes, its temples and triumphs, we should quote here an irreverent but probably accurate account of daily life there in about 200 BC by the comic playwright Plautus, in his play *Curculio* (*The Weevil*, or *The Parasite*). He conjures up an image not of serious Roman statesmen pontificating in the Senate or law courts but of the colourful low life to be found in different parts of the Forum:

*If a man wants to meet a perjurer, let him go to the Comitium [where politicians made speeches], and if he wants to meet a liar or a braggart, he should go to the temple of Venus Cloacina [the Shrine of Cloacina, identified with Venus, in front of the Basilica Aemilia]; for married men who waste their money let him ask at the Basilica [Aemilia]. There too he will find 'mature' prostitutes and men who are accustomed to quoting a price, while at the Forum fish market he'll find those who are devotees of public feasts. In the lower Forum good and well-to-do men stroll up and down; in the middle forum near the Canal [Cloaca Maxima], the mere show-offs; above the lake [Lacus Curtius] are those insolent, garrulous, and nasty types who audaciously slander others for no reason and who themselves have plenty that one could quite truthfully criticise. Beneath the Old Shops [on the site of the future Basilica Julia] are those who loan and borrow money at interest. Behind the temple of Castor [and Pollux], there you will find those whom you shouldn't believe too quickly. In the Vicus*

*Tuscus [Tuscan Street, next to the Temple of Castor and Pollux]
are the men who sell themselves.*

Because today the Forum seems to have no function other than to serve mass tourism, and certainly contains nothing of any interest for sale, it is virtually impossible to reconstruct in one's mind the lively place evoked by Plautus when one visits what is now, despite fragments of major buildings, a place of dust, ugly foundations and incomprehensible lumps of brick. We need to recall such vivid images as that of Suetonius when he describes how the Emperor Claudius, despite his attempts to ensure the corn supply for the citizens of Rome, was 'once stopped in the middle of the Forum by a mob and so pelted with abuse and at the same time with pieces of bread that he was hardly able to escape to the Palace by a back door'. Suetonius also records of Nero that 'right in the Roman Forum he gouged out the eye of a Roman knight for being too outspoken in chiding him'. Julia, the sexually driven daughter of dignified Augustus, was accused of having taken part in orgies in the Forum, soliciting passers-by like a prostitute, while her husband, Emperor Tiberius, was absent in Rhodes. Even with the most powerful imagination, we can hardly envisage the city-scape of the once-busy Forum, criss-crossed by roads of which little more than confusing sections and their names now survive: Vicus Jugarius, Vicus Tuscus, Via Nova, Via Sacra, the route of the last of these, though vitally important, still uncertain.

In the next chapter we shall shed light on this tangle by exploring the Forum and the monuments of its imperial age with Piranesi, perhaps the greatest topographical artist of all time, as our guide.

..................................................................................................

# VISITING THE ANCIENT BUILDINGS
# WITH PIRANESI

There is no better introduction to the ancient Roman buildings in the Forum than the engravings of Giovanni Battista
Piranesi (1720–78), who went so far as to claim – echoing the
Roman poet Horace's boast that he was leaving the world 'a
monument more lasting than bronze' (*monumentum aere per-
ennius*)– that, 'I do dare to believe that, like Horace, I have executed a work which will go down to posterity, and which will
endure for as long as there are men desirous of knowing all that
has survived till our day of the ruins of the most famous city of
the universe.' Let us, therefore, take him at his word and allow
him to act as our guide when making our tour of the Forum.
What kind of Forum do Piranesi's engravings represent? The
answer is that they are the best record of the buildings erected
in the Rome of the emperors from Augustus onwards. It is
important to stress this because, although most visitors come
with the great politicians and orators of the Republic in their
minds, such as Julius Caesar and Cicero, no monuments from
that period have survived for either us or Piranesi to observe.
Even those buildings, like the Temples of Castor and Pollux or
of Saturn, whose origins go back to early in the Republic, are
now known only in a much later imperial form.

One of Piranesi's models was the numerous surviving fragments of the Marble Plan of Rome, a remarkable map of the city that was inscribed for the Emperor Septimius Severus (reigned AD 193–211). Eighteen metres high and thirteen wide, it was originally displayed on a wall at the Temple of Peace, now part of the church of SS. Cosmas and Damian in the Forum. No similar plan survives of any other Roman city, though we know that some were made, so this constitutes one of the most powerful and unusual testimonies to the huge political and cultural significance which the Romans attached to the urban forms of their capital city. It was unequalled until the great scale model of Rome in the time of Constantine was completed in 1937 to almost the same scale as the Marble Plan, of which only 10 per cent survives today. The stunning scale model gathers dust in the little-visited Museo della Cività Romana, which is disliked by modern Romans because it was commissioned by Mussolini.

A genius of intense and passionate character, Piranesi produced over a thousand etchings, which were better engraved, printed on finer paper and larger – some of them two feet wide – than any by his contemporaries. They included twenty-five views of the Forum: four in his *Alcune vedute di Archi Trionfali, ed altri monumenti* (*Some Views of Triumphal Arches and Other Monuments*) and nine in his *Antichità Romane* (*Roman Antiquities*). These were surpassed in quality by the more gripping fourteen of the Forum in his *Vedute di Roma* (*Views of Rome*), nearly 140 plates published gradually from 1748 to 1778. Of these fourteen, eight are reproduced as illustrations in the present book. His visionary yet accurate depictions frequently depended on the use of a complete panoramic spread of 180 degrees and an imaginary viewpoint

*5. View from the centre of the Forum (Piranesi, Vedute di Roma, c. 1748–78).*
In the foreground is the fountain and handsome water trough of 1593 sadly
removed to the Piazza de Quirinale by Pope Pius VII in 1818. The three
columns of the temple of Castor and Pollux frame the now demolished
church of Sta Maria Liberatrice. The elm avenue leads towards S. Francesca
Romana and its convent buildings which swallow up the Arch of Titus.

far above ground level. It is as though a modern film camera has swept across the scene, an effect easily appreciated in his two greatest views of the Forum, looking east, one showing its length from the Arch of Septimius Severus to the Arch of Titus (fig. 1), the other looking from a point near its middle by the Temple of Castor and Pollux (fig. 5).

Piranesi's view of the full length of the Forum (fig. 1) is believed to have been taken from a still-existing window in the Palazzo Senatorio in the Piazza del Campidoglio on the Capitol, a building serving the same function today as it has for centuries, housing the city council of Rome. From the terrace at the south side of the Palazzo Senatorio, the modern visitor can enjoy a similar view to Piranesi's, but it now includes nineteenth- and twentieth-century reconstructions of ancient buildings, notably the Portico of Harmonious Gods, the Rostra, the Temple of Divus Julius, the Shrine of Juturna, the Temple of Vesta and the Arch of Titus. We shall explore these reconstructions, as well as the Early Christian, Renaissance, and Baroque buildings that Piranesi did not illustrate, in later chapters.

Piranesi always described himself as an architect, though only one building was ever put up from his designs: S. Maria del Priorato on the Aventine Hill in Rome. Rather over-loaded with crisp symbolical ornament, its façade ends up looking more like an engraving than a building. Nonetheless, the vision of antiquity celebrated in his engravings was intended to inspire modern architects to produce buildings of a power and grandeur similar to those of the ancients. He hailed as someone who could achieve this ambition the British architect Robert Adam, who studied the monuments of ancient Rome with him from 1755 to 1757. Adam in turn described Piranesi as the Italian artist who might be said most completely 'to breathe the ancient air', as well as 'the most extraordinary fellow I ever saw', though he complained that 'his ideas in locution [are] so ill arranged, his expression so furious and fantastic'.

Piranesi recorded the monuments before the age of archaeology, when, in the nineteenth and twentieth centuries, as we shall see, some of them were reconstituted in new versions that visitors now so often assume to be authentically antique. He is thus an excellent guide today, because any ancient building he shows we can take as genuinely ancient. Moreover, virtually no large-scale monuments of importance have been discovered in the Forum since his day. We should also be grateful that Piranesi recorded what he called 'these speaking ruins' in the Forum at the last point at which they still made it one of the most beautiful and evocative places in the world, accompanied by the refreshing trickle of water at the great drinking fountain and the no less welcome shade of the elm avenue, both facilities alas long vanished. Exactly ten years after Piranesi's death, the first of the militant archaeologists arrived with his pickaxe, the Swede Carl Fredenheim. In later chapters we shall investigate the Forum after a further two and a quarter centuries of the victory of the pickaxe.

Piranesi's engravings repay detailed study, for he took delight in the contrast between the timeless ruins, encrusted with feathery weeds, and the modern life around them, including tumble-down stables, carts, massive oxen, wiry goats, pack-horses and yapping dogs. The pictures are also alive with a small army of peasants, beggars, cripples, shepherds, labourers and tradesmen, while ladies and gentleman of a higher social status disport themselves just below the capitals of the largely buried Temple of Vespasian (fig. 14), all humans being drawn deliberately small to emphasise the grandeur of the architecture.

However, we should not be deceived into seeing his work as just a light-hearted, late-Rococo fantasy. As we have noted, Piranesi was, above all, an architect with a mission. In the dedication to his very first book, the *Prima Parte di Architettura e Prospettive* (1743) (*First Part of Architecture and Perspective*), he had explained that his engravings of the public buildings and ruined structures of the ancient Romans were intended to reprove the mediocrity of contemporary architecture. Believing that he had a mission to reform modern architecture, which he regarded as debased, he memorably recorded that 'These speaking ruins have filled my "spirit" with images that accurate drawings, even such as those of the immortal Palladio, could never have succeeded in conveying.' Before we begin our investigation of the Forum, we should be warned that Piranesi's engravings made such a powerful impact on visitors such as Goethe and Flaxman that they confessed finding the actual ruins disappointing in comparison.

## ARCH OF SEPTIMIUS SEVERUS

In Piranesi's principal general view of the Forum (fig. 1) we begin on the left-hand side in the foreground with the gigantic Arch of Septimius Severus, then nearly half buried. On its left and right sides, the top of the side-arches of this vast triple-arched structure are just visible. Originally seventy-five feet high and eighty-two feet wide, it was built in AD 203 to celebrate the victories of the African-born Emperor Severus and his sons, Caracalla and Geta, against the Parthians in

6. *Column of Phocas, Arch of Septimius Severus, and SS. Luca e Martina* *(Piranesi,* Vedute di Roma, c. *1748–78).* On the left is the back of the Palazzo Senatorio on the Capitol. In the foreground is the Column of Phocas but the high soil level has buried the marble pedestal surmounting the pyramid of steps on which it rests. The Arch of Septimius Severus also awaits excavation. Pietro da Cortona's magnificent church of SS. Luca e Martina with its curved façade is in the incomplete state in which it remained until the adjacent houses were demolished in 1932 to excavate the remains of ancient Roman foundations.

what we would call the near East including the modern Iran. It is a tremendously florid arch (though a yet more florid one was erected in Severus' honour in his birthplace of Lepcis Magna in modern Libya), for a luckless family: in 208 Severus went with his sons to Britain, where he died at Eboracum (York) three years later. Caracalla and Geta succeeded him as joint emperors but Caracalla murdered Geta in 212 and was himself murdered in 217.

Piranesi included the Arch of Septimius Severus in several other engravings of the Forum (fig. 6). For him, as for us, the triumphal arch was one of the most characteristic inventions of the ancient Romans, its sole function being an awesome celebration of power and military might. Recent work on the roof of this arch has revealed traces of a vast bronze triumphal chariot that once stood where Piranesi pictures just a few weeds. It has sometimes been wrongly claimed that chariots could not pass through the central arch because it was approached up steps, but this error arose when archaeologists at the beginning of the twentieth century demolished the road running through it and contemporary with it to expose the earlier Augustan road at a lower level.

The arch was primarily a monument of display, a support not only for the chariot on top but also for the lavish sculptures, now much corroded by diesel fumes but recently cleaned, depicting the victorious campaigns. In the nineteenth century, it was a form eagerly adopted by the imperialists of Europe when echoes of the Arch of Septimius Severus, as well as that of Constantine (which stands between the Forum and the Colosseum), were built in cities such as Berlin, Paris, London and Brussels.

Looking closely, we can see that Piranesi has carefully

detailed the free-standing columns of white marble, four on each side. These are in the Composite order which, like the triumphal arch as a building type, is a characteristically Roman invention. It piles Ionic volutes on top of the bell formed by the acanthus leaves of the Corinthian order in a not entirely convincing attempt to create a new order – and to demonstrate that the Romans were as architecturally inventive as the Greeks, who had devised the Doric, Ionic and Corinthian orders between the sixth and fifth centuries BC.

The core of the Arch of Septimius Severus is of travertine and brick, but this has a facing of marble, every inch of which is decorated with a rich fretwork of carving: as well as the panels depicting Severus' eastern campaigns, more easily visible now at eye level are the expressive figures of Roman soldiers with Parthian captives that are carved on the tall bases – technically the dados – on which the columns rest. The theme of overall sculptural adornment is continued in a different mode on the panels on both faces of the attic, which are filled with the elegant but densely packed lettering of carved dedicatory inscriptions. The letters were originally filled with gilt bronze, and there was further gilt bronze adornment in the form of statues, trophies and garlands, all of which has now disappeared. Four small rooms within this attic were approached by a staircase leading up within the south pier.

In the Middle Ages, the arch was divided between two owners: the little church of SS. Sergio e Bacco was attached to it on the south side, and the north side was used as part of a fortress by a Roman baronial family who erected a tower on top of it.

Since the identification of this building as the Senate House (Curia) in 1860, it has been for visitors one of the most important buildings in the Forum, despite its plain exterior. Piranesi, for whom it was simply 'Treasury, today church of S. Adriano', included it in only one of his twenty-five views of the Forum (fig. 1), in which it is largely hidden by the far more splendid Arch of Septimius Severus which he rightly preferred. S. Adriano, which was built inside the Senate House, had a splendid Baroque interior which, as we shall see in Chapter 4, was destroyed in the twentieth century.

The Senate House itself, a rather bleak rectangular structure, was built very late in the Empire during the reigns of Diocletian and Maximian (AD 284–305) as part of the reconstruction of the Forum after the fire of AD 283. Though large, it is not especially imposing; but, like the earlier Senate House which it replaced, it had a now-lost colonnade without a pediment along its entrance front. Also, with its brick façades originally faced with stucco, its appearance would have been a little grander than it seems to either Piranesi or the modern visitor.

The Senate House had been founded on this site by Julius Caesar to replace the Republican version which stood a little to the west. It is deeply characteristic of a place with as long a history as the Forum, where nothing is what it seems to be on the surface, that the present Senate House was not the one in which the great debates of Roman senators took place during the Republic, when Rome became established as a world power. In fact, it was a reconstruction erected in the late empire, when the role of the Senate was somewhat ambiguous. Indeed, from the time of Trajan (reigned AD 98–117), there was little real political life here, for the Emperor was all. The Senate House we see now was not the place where Cicero railed against Catiline, but where senators debated topics such as whether to remove the Altar of Victory set up by Augustus. Diocletian's decision to rebuild the Senate House on the existing foundations and to the same dimensions can be compared to Winston Churchill's decision to rebuild on the old lines the British House of Commons after bomb damage in the Second World War: both were gestures of respectful conservatism.

The bronze entrance doors, which were left open during debates, are copies, the originals having been taken by the leading architect of Baroque Rome, Francesco Borromini, to the main portal of the cathedral of Rome, the historic papal basilica of St John Lateran, where they still survive. Internally the building relied for its effect on its rich pavement of coloured marbles, still visible, and on now lost marble and mosaic facings on the walls. It contained five rows of chairs for 300 senators; the steps on either side where they voted remain intact, and the setting has been re-created in many modern films.

## TEMPLE OF ANTONINUS AND FAUSTINA

Piranesi was rightly devoted to this building, which boasts the most complete surviving portico of any temple in the Forum. He thus included it in four engravings, even devoting a separate one to it alone (fig. 2). One's attention concentrates on the eye-catching portico of Carystian green marble, six columns wide and three deep at the ends, which was originally approached exclusively up a flight of ten steps, provision for disabled access being unknown in the Roman Empire. Piranesi could not show these steps because, along with the lower section of the columns, they were buried beneath the accumulation of earth and rubbish, six metres deep which, well before his time, had already covered the original ground level of the Forum. When Orazio Torriani built S. Lorenzo in Miranda within the temple in 1601, its entrance door was, of course, at the then ground level, but is today stranded almost half way up the façade, now that archaeologists have lowered the floor of the Forum to its ancient Roman level. Since the reason for this peculiarity is not explained in guidebooks, visitors will be baffled by it. The approach to the portico also suffers today from the loss of the podium arms, the low walls which would have protected the sides of the steps leading up to it and would also have made the front of the temple less disengaged than it now appears.

Piranesi's view reveals it as a piece of frontal display, for, despite its impressive entrance portico, it has no columns at all on its side or rear walls. However, richness is provided by the frieze on the sides, which is boldly carved with huge scrolls of acanthus leaves, sacrificial vessels and pairs of griffins, sacred to Apollo, facing each other. The dedication of the temple refers to Emperor Antoninus Pius (reigned AD 138–61) and his wife, Faustina, who died in AD 140 near the beginning of his reign which, for a Roman Emperor, was exceptionally peaceful. He began it in her memory in the year of her death. The entablature on the entrance front bears the dedicatory inscription, DIVAE FAUSTINAE EX S.C. ('To Deified Faustina, by decree of the Senate'). After the death of Antoninus, the words DIVO ANTONINO ET ('To Deified Antoninus and') were added above.

Characteristically for many Roman temples, it was a

retrospective building, its plan looking back to the temples of the Augustan era at the end of the first century BC, and its decoration to the Temple of Vespasian of about a century later. Its portico reflected the more recent Pantheon built by Hadrian in AD *c.* 118–*c.* 128, the shafts of the columns of both porticoes being the same height (40 feet) and the details of their bases virtually identical.

In one of his views, Piranesi shows the south side of the Forum bordered by a row of modern houses leading from the Senate House to the Temple of Antoninus and Faustina. The portico of this temple can be seen on the edge of the Forum below the tall, pedimented façade of the church of S. Lorenzo, which, as we have noted, was built by Torriani within the temple. Though Piranesi shows the exterior of Torriani's church, slotted into the temple, he did not illustrate its interior, which survives today; like the interior of the Senate House, we shall describe it in Chapter 4.

## 'TEMPLE OF ROMULUS'

In Piranesi's general views of the Forum (figs. 1 and 5), we can see next to the Temple of Antoninus and Faustina the modest, circular 'Temple of Romulus', or 'Divus Romulus', which survives today, though without the prominent cupola shown in these views. It is doubtful whether it was a temple, and it is certain that it had nothing to do with Romulus, the mythical co-founder of Rome. Dating from the early fourth century AD, it is traditionally associated with the son of the Emperor Maxentius (reigned AD 306–12), who was called Romulus but died aged four in AD 309, at which point he was deified, hence the name 'Divus Romulus'.

A brick-faced concrete building with a concrete dome, the 'Temple of Romulus' incorporates elements brought from earlier buildings. Known as *spolia*, this re-use of early fragments was to become characteristic of Roman work of this late date, notably in Early Christian buildings. At the 'Temple of Romulus', the bronze doors and their marble frame were brought from a Severan building of AD *c.* 200, while the flanking columns of red porphyry and the carved lintel over them came from other sources. The building was flanked by two long apsidal halls, now largely disappeared save for the two Carystian green marble columns, also *spolia*, of the right-hand porch.

Above the cupola of this 'temple' we can see in Piranesi's engravings the pedimented upper half of the Early Christian church of SS. Cosmas and Damian. This began life as a great hall in the ancient Roman Temple of Peace, to which it was probably designed as an entrance from the Via Sacra. The circular form of this 'temple' cleverly masks the fact that the hall lies at an oblique angle to the street. (The architect and town-planner John Nash, faced with a similar problem in Regent Street, London, around 1,500 years later, adopted the same solution by giving his church of All Souls, Langham Place, a circular tower behind which the nave runs away at an angle.) When the hall was remodelled as SS. Cosmas and Damian, the 'Temple of Romulus' became its entrance vestibule from the Forum. The church, its interior unillustrated by Piranesi, will be considered in Chapter 4.

Piranesi manages to fit in the small Oratorio degli Amanti di Gesù e Maria al Monte Calvario (Oratory of the Lovers of Jesus and Mary on Mount Calvary), squeezed in on a wedge-shaped site next to the 'Temple of Romulus'. Built under

Pope Benedict XIV in the mid eighteenth century for an arch-confraternity of priests, this small church was the start of processions along the Via Sacra to the nearby Colosseum, which had been restored by Benedict, where the priests had a series of small shrines. Following its needless demolition in the name of archaeology in 1877, this church has entirely vanished from architectural history and is not mentioned in accounts of the Forum. However, Piranesi clearly shows its classical façade, with pilasters below a curved pediment, and its long roof running back to the church of SS. Cosmas and Damian. There is a fuller record of it in an enchanting panorama of the Forum (in the Victoria and Albert Museum) painted by Ludovico Carraciolo in 1824.

### BASILICA OF MAXENTIUS

Piranesi shows the three, colossal coffered arches of the Basilica of Maxentius, still misidentified in his day as the Temple of Peace, using rich shadow and strong sunlight to emphasise their depth and strength (fig. 7). This grandeur contrasts with the tiny figures in the foreground, including a horse and cart, leaving us in no doubt that this is the most magnificent building in the Forum: as we shall see, it has some claim to be one of the 'Wonders of the World'. However, it is not always easy to visit it because it is laid out in the summer with chairs and equipment for concerts, a tradition begun under Mussolini in 1933. Since to see even its exterior, screened by trees, it is necessary to make a detour off the Via Sacra, it is possible that many visitors will leave the Forum without realising that it is there! It seems to have been begun by Maxentius immediately after a great fire of AD 307. The last pagan emperor to

7. *Basilica of Maxentius (Piranesi,* Vedute di Roma, c. *1748–78).* This vast
building housing law courts was begun by Maxentius in *c.* AD 306–7 and
completed from *c.* AD 313 by Constantine. It survived largely intact until the
thirteenth century after which an earthquake reduced it to the state shown
by Piranesi in whose day it was wrongly identified as the Templum Pacis
(Temple of Peace).

choose Rome as his capital, his basilica was completed from AD 313 by Constantine the Great, even though he had already defeated him in military conflict.

This vast rectangular building incorporating law courts had a broad central nave, running north–south, flanked on each side by an aisle of the same width, but this nave was bisected by an identical nave and aisles running east–west. One wonders how all these extensive spaces were used, but it should be noted that at the beginning of the fourth century the building became the judicial seat of the prefecture in charge of the administrative functions of the city. The interior was, unusually, single-storeyed, unlike the two-storeyed basilicas Aemilia and Julia in the Forum. It was also the first basilica to be vaulted throughout, making it fireproof. As planned and built by Maxentius, its axis ran east–west, with the entrance portico on the east front and an apse in the central bay of the west front. At the time of Constantine or probably later, at the end of the fourth century AD, its size was increased when its axis was turned through a right angle to create a sumptuous new entrance on the south front in the Via Sacra and also a new apse in the middle of the north side.

Constantine used the western apse to house a colossal statue of himself, which, for a Christian emperor, was curiously like the cult statue of a god in a temple, both in its vast height of thirty feet and in its remote and hieratic facial expression (fig. 8). Discovered in 1487, it is now thought that the re-worked head must originally have represented Maxentius. Substantial fragments of this white marble colossus, including the head, eight feet six inches high, survive in the courtyard of the Palazzo dei Conservatori on the Capitoline Hill.

8. *Head of the statue of Constantine from the Basilica of Maxentius.* Parts of this white marble colossus, originally thirty feet high, survive in the courtyard of the Palazzo dei Conservatori on the Capitoline Hill. The overpowering head of Constantine, eight feet six inches high, is dated to *c.* AD 313, though it is possibly a later replacement.

This monumentality also characterised the Basilica of Maxentius itself, as can be appreciated by what survives today, the whole of the north aisle with its central apse and its three arched exedrae with giant coffered barrel vaults which served to buttress the central groin-vaulted nave. It is built of brick-faced concrete, the inner walls lined with marble. The arches are eighty feet high and sixty-seven feet wide, the same width as those in St Peter's, for it was a powerful source of inspiration for Bramante. The nave, 115 feet high (higher than that in Westminster Abbey), was inspired in design and construction by the system of concrete vaults that had previously been used only for the central halls of the imperial baths, notably those in Rome of Caracalla and Diocletian. Indeed, probably inspired by the Great Hall of the contemporary Baths of Diocletian, the Basilica of Maxentius may have been designed by the same architect who here solved the problem of how to span a triple nave with a vault (fig. 9).

Concrete, increasingly used by the Romans from at the latest the second century BC, was made from mortar mixed with slaked lime and a kind of crushed volcanic rock found both at Puteoli (Pozzuoli), near Naples, and also near Rome. This created a compact, monolithic mass which was as strong as it was durable. As the elder Pliny observed, 'one cannot marvel enough' at concrete, though the Basilica of Maxentius was built too late to be mentioned in much Latin literature. Unlike architects in the modern world, the Roman architects wisely chose not to expose concrete surfaces but rather covered them with marble, mosaic or brick.

Interestingly, for his churches Constantine eschewed the masonry vaults of such buildings for the unadventurous flat wooden ceilings of earlier basilicas. However, the staggering

9. *Basilica of Maxentius (reconstruction painting, William Suddaby).* This shows the massive but now lost cross vaults, rising 115 feet above the marble floor. One of the great spaces of the ancient world, it was inspired by the similar halls in the imperial Roman baths. In the western apse is the colossal seated statue of Constantine set up by that emperor in a bold secular imitation of the practice of the ancient Greeks who housed enormous cult statues of gods in their temples.

technical achievement of buildings like the Basilica of Maxentius was one of the reasons why the Romans were venerated until the nineteenth century as having surpassed the modern world in architecture and engineering as well as in the construction of roads, bridges and aqueducts. The great domed church of Sta Sophia, Constantinople, built by Emperor Justinian in the AD 530s, rivals the scale of the Basilica of Maxentius, which its principal architect, Anthemios of Tralles, may well have seen. Apart from this, vaults on the scale of those in the Basilica of Maxentius were not to be built for another 700 years. In attempting to understand Roman monumentality, the Basilica provides the most important evidence, a fact which alone makes the Forum a place of fundamental significance. This was surely one of the major buildings of the world.

The building survived largely intact until the thirteenth century but was gravely damaged in the earthquake of 1349. We can still appreciate its scale but less easily the lavish polychromy of its vanished interior decoration, including the walls with coloured marble revetments, and the vast, geometrically patterned floor of red and green porphyry and different marbles – Numidian yellow, Carystian green and Phrygian purple. It is impossible to overstate the enormous change such use of marble during the Empire made to the appearance of the Forum, which, in its Republican days had been of rough tufa. Since so little survives of the original materials from either period, we tend to ignore the contrast, while acknowledging that marble was sometimes used even in the Republican period.

At the Basilica of Maxentius we have also lost the fluted Corinthian columns, forty-seven feet high, of Proconnesian

10. *Temple of Venus and Roma, perspective view from north-east (Piranesi, Vedute di Roma, c. 1748–78)*. Most of what Piranesi illustrates survives intact today, though he was unaware that it formed part of Hadrien's great temple as altered by Maxentius. As usual, he enjoyed depicting modern life beneath the ruins: here a Benedictine monk from the Convent of S. Francesca Romana, built into the temple, is seen in front of a washing line hung with items of ecclesiastical laundry

marble from the Sea of Marmora. These appeared to carry the vaults, though these were in fact supported by the concrete-cored piers to which they were attached. Thus, in characteristically Roman fashion, the columns were essentially decoration. One of them was removed by Pope Paul V in 1613 to adorn the Piazza outside the Basilica of Sta Maria Maggiore, where, crowned by the Pope with a statue of the Virgin, it can still be admired.

## TEMPLE OF VENUS AND ROMA

Adjacent to the Basilica of Maxentius on the east was the Temple of Venus and Roma, to which Piranesi devoted a spectacular plate, though he did not include it in his two general views of the Forum because he wrongly regarded it as an outlying part of the vast Golden House of Nero on the adjacent Esquiline (fig. 10). He stressed its tall, powerful, and diagonally coffered apse by depicting it in the bright sunlight of Rome, contrasting with the deep black shadow behind it from which emerges a barrel vault filled with rectangular coffering. Most of the antique buildings in the Forum are too ruinous to have retained their interiors, so this temple was of special interest to Piranesi, as it was to other architects before and after him, who used it as a model for modern buildings.

The Temple of Venus and Roma was begun by Hadrian in AD 125–6 on the Velia, the low hill between the Forum and the Colosseum. It was built on the site of the vestibule of the Golden House, where Nero had put a colossal bronze statue of himself as the Sun. This had to be removed to accommodate the temple (fig. 35). Like Vespasian's nearby Colosseum,

Hadrian's temple could thus be seen as an imperial demonstration of magnificence for the public rather than of private indulgence and vanity. It certainly conformed with the claim he had made at the start of his reign that he would govern the state so that all would know it belonged to the people, not to him alone.

Hadrian had clearly intended to plant a Greek temple in the heart of Rome. It is not always sufficiently stressed that many emperors, including Claudius, Nero, Titus, Domitian and Hadrian himself, were passionate Graecophiles. Hadrian's Temple of Venus and Roma was probably started, or at least vowed, on 21 April AD 121, the 'birthday of Rome'. He visited Athens and the Peloponnese three years later, while at his celebrated villa at Tivoli near Rome, which he laid out as a theatre of memory, he even built a Greek Revival Temple of Aphrodite in the Doric order. He spent more than twelve years of his 21-year reign away from Rome, often making his visits for cultural rather than military purposes.

The most important of the Greek elements of the Temple of Venus and Roma was that it was not raised on the customary high Roman podium but on a low stylobate with a continuous colonnade, so that it was accessible from all four sides. In this it recalled the giant Temple of Olympian Zeus in Athens, where in AD 129 Hadrian dedicated the shrine of Zeus that he had commissioned.

With the possible exception of the Temple of Serapis on the Quirinal Hill, Hadrian's Temple of Venus and Roma was larger than any other in Rome, including the Pantheon and the Temple of Jupiter Capitolinus. The height of its columns, fifty feet, was only equalled at the Temple of Mars Ultor of 37–2 BC in the Forum of Augustus. Probably dedicated between AD 135 and 137, Hadrian's temple seems to have been completed in AD 140–45 by his successor, Antoninus Pius.

Hadrian inventively linked the cults of two divinities that reflected different religious aspects of Rome: Venus, as the mother of Rome, through Aeneas, was naturally a popular goddess, while Roma was the official god of the city. Moreover, the particular Venus venerated here was Venus Felix, a goddess of fecundity and prosperity who was unknown before the time of Hadrian, while Roma was also an innovative choice for, though she had been worshipped in the Greek East as a political act of homage from the second century BC, she was not taken up in Rome until relatively late. In stressing Rome rather than the imperial family, Hadrian's temple, which was accompanied by a new annual celebration of the foundation of Rome, Natalis Urbis Romae, had a national rather than a dynastic character.

The novelty does not end here. Hadrian, a noted architectural amateur, must surely have been responsible for the unique plan of this double temple, in which the cult figures of the two goddesses were placed back to back in two separate temple spaces, or cellas (fig. 11). According to an extraordinary and somewhat improbable story told by Dio Cassius, Hadrian sent his plans for the temple to the architect Apollodorus of Damascus for his opinion. Apollodorus unwisely made a number of criticisms, including that it was too Greek and that the cult statues were too tall for the cellas because Hadrian had followed Greek practice, in which the statues were always enormous. Hadrian accordingly had the poor man put to death. After a fire in AD 307, the temple was transformed internally by Maxentius, who replaced its Grecian character with Roman magnificence when he replaced the

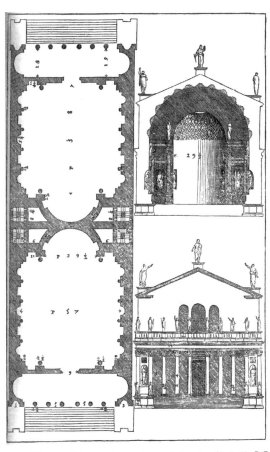

11. *Temple of Venus and Roma, plan, section and elevation (Palladio,* I Quattro
Libri dell'Architettura, *1570).* Hadrian's great temple, vowed in AD 121, was
identified by Palladio as 'the Temples of the Sun and Moon in the garden of
S. Maria Nova [S. Francesca Romana].' He explained that, 'I have designed
the loggias in front and the decoration inside as I imagined they would have
been.' The twin apses, with their influential lozenge-shaped coffering, were
part of the rebuilding by Maxentius after the fire of AD 307.

wooden roofs of the two cellas with giant coffered apses and concrete vaults. He also doubled the depth of the wall mass to carry the weight of the new work.

The western end of the site is now occupied by the church of S. Francesca Romana, as we shall see in Chapter 4, but a significant portion of the Temple of Venus and Roma as remodelled by Maxentius survives today, notably the giant apses of the two cellas, their semi-domes filled with diamond-shaped coffering. More survives of the western, Roma, cella, which boasts a marble floor and porphyry columns as well as its great south wall, capped by a portion of its coffered barrel vault. Piranesi chose to record this coffering and the eastern Venus cella in his engraving. The western apse, later enclosed within the conventual buildings of S. Francesca Romana, can be seen from a room in the convent, now the Antiquarium Forense. We shall note in the final chapter the improvements made under Mussolini to the presentation of the temple.

Since the interiors of few ancient Roman buildings survived intact to serve as models to post-antique architects, the coffered semi-domes of the temple were frequently echoed on a smaller scale from the Renaissance till modern times. An early example is in the portico of the neo-antique Palazzo Massimo alle Colonne, Rome (1532–7), by Baldassare Peruzzi, whose example was followed by Lord Burlington in the gallery of his neo-Palladian Villa at Chiswick (*c.* 1725–9).

ARCH OF TITUS

Piranesi made unforgettable engravings of the east and west fronts of the Arch of Titus. It was built in AD 81–2 but later incorporated into medieval fortifications and monastic

12. *Arch of Titus, west front (Piranesi,* Vedute di Roma, c. *1748–78).* Piranesi's
richly detailed scene of life in the Forum shows how little was left of the
Arch of Titus by his time. Of the four Composite columns originally on this
front only half of two survived and the whole carved attic had gone. All of
this was replaced by Stern and Valadier in 1819–22 when they dismantled the
arch, making it effectively a nineteenth-century monument, except for the
sculptural reliefs.

buildings, into which Piranesi shows it still incorporated (fig. 12). He seemed to enjoy depicting its spectacular decay, with its outer columns missing and its inner ones surviving to little more than half their original height. In what could be an illustration to Gibbon's *Decline and Fall of the Roman Empire*, he revels in its incongruous juxtaposition with the wooden gates of what he unexpectedly identifies in the caption as a 'polveriere' (powder magazine), sheltered by a pair of twisted trees. Since the time of Piranesi, the columns have been repaired or replaced and all the later additions demolished, so that the arch is today a free-standing monument as it was in antiquity. However, as we shall see in Chapter 6, its rebuilding in the early nineteenth century means that, except for its sculpture, much of it is now modern (fig. 34).

The arch commanded a splendid view over the rooftops of the Forum to the Temple of Jupiter Capitolinus, the goal of triumphal processions, below which could be seen the temple dedicated to Vespasian and his son Titus. One of the purest of all triumphal arches, the Arch of Titus was constructed of Attic marble from Mount Pentelicon, though its columns were in the Roman Composite order. As we have seen at the Arch of Septimius Severus, by yoking together the defining features of the two richest Greek orders, Ionic and Corinthian, the Composite seemed to represent the triumph of Rome over Greece. This order may have been invented for Augustus, but it was given special expression by Vespasian and his sons, Titus and Domitian. Though this belief in Roman superiority was a very different vision from that of Hadrian, it was bolstered by the writings of the elder Piny, who had recently described arches as a modern invention.

Dedicated to the memory of Titus by his brother and

successor, Domitian (reigned AD 81–96), the Arch of Titus commemorates the conquest by Titus of the Jewish revolt and his destruction of Jerusalem in AD 70. It is decorated with some of the most compelling narrative scenes in the history of Roman sculpture, leading the poet Shelley to observe that here 'is sculptured, in deep relief, the desolation of a city'. The deified figure of Titus, who died in AD 81, is depicted rising to heaven on the back of an eagle, in a panel where the nine central coffers on the underside of the archway would normally be, while both flanks of this inside tunnel of the arch are carved with reliefs of scenes from the triumphs, which had been accorded by the Senate in AD 71 to Titus and his father, Vespasian.

On the south side, we see the procession from the Campus Martius to the Capitoline Hill as it passes the site of the future Arch of Titus. In these dramatic and convincingly illusionistic scenes we seem to be in the procession ourselves, watching the young soldiers, crowned with laurel wreaths, carrying a litter bearing booty from the Great Temple at Jerusalem, which had been sacked in the Jewish war (fig. 13). Prominent is the menorah, the seven-branched golden candelabrum, which was the most sacred object owned by the Jews. It was believed to be the one recorded in Exodus as made for Moses in accordance with instructions from God. Installed by Solomon in the Temple of Solomon in Jerusalem, the largest temple in the world, the menorah was taken by Titus, along with other ceremonial objects of silver and gold from the temple, to Vespasian's Templum Pacis (Temple of Peace), next to the Forum. These precious objects are all now lost and have not been seen since AD 614. According to Simon Goldhill, this loss, together with the destruction of the

Temple of Jerusalem by Titus (though possibly not intended by him), 'has made the Arch a necessary stop for tourists to Rome in a way that the emperor could never have expected. What was meant to be a monument to Titus's everlasting military glory has become an icon of the enduring symbolic power of the destroyed Temple of the Jews.' Nonetheless, until the practice was discontinued by Pope Pius IX in 1846, a Jew was obliged to stand by the arch and swear loyalty to the Pope as his procession passed through it on the occasion of his installation.

In the relief on the north side of the archway we see Titus (though the image of his head has long since been destroyed) driving in a chariot accompanied by the goddess Roma. A female figure of Victory holds a wreath over his head, and his official attendants, the lictors, carry their fasces, or sacrificial axes. The People of Rome are represented by a partially nude figure, and the Senate by one wearing a toga. On the west and east fronts of the arch the spandrels on either side of the opening are filled with sprawling figures, flying winged Victories carrying banners, trophies, laurel wreaths and palm branches. There was originally even more sculpture: the arch was surmounted by a bronze quadriga, that is, a four-horse chariot and driver, here containing Vespasian and Titus. The combination of real figures with divine ones, though already a feature of some Roman art, was new on the ambitious scale of the Arch of Titus and was influential on the development of sculpture.

The monumental *History of the Jewish Wars*, written in Greek by the Jewish statesman and soldier Flavius Josephus in the first century AD, contains a rapturous account of the triumphal procession of Vespasian through the city of Rome

13. *Arch of Titus, sculptural relief in the passage way*. Built in AD 81–2, the arch was dedicated to the memory of Titus by his brother and successor, Domitian (AD 81–96). Since it commemorated the victories of Titus and Vespasian in the Jewish Wars and the destruction of Jerusalem by Titus in AD 70, this scene shows soldiers parading through the arch, bearing spoils which include the seven-branched Menorah from the Temple of Jerusalem.

and the Forum to celebrate the capture of Jerusalem. It was after this that Vespasian decided to build the Temple of Peace on the northern edge of the Forum, in which sumptuous building, Josephus tells us, he housed the treasures of the Temple of Jerusalem.

## TEMPLE OF CASTOR AND POLLUX

On the right or south side of the Forum, Piranesi shows (figs. 1 and 5) the long boundary wall of the Farnese Gardens and the church of S. Maria Liberatrice, but since both of these date from the sixteenth and seventeenth centuries and no longer survive we shall consider them in Chapters 4 and 5 respectively. We pass now to the three surviving columns of the Temple of Castor and Pollux near the centre of the Forum on its south side (figs. 5 and 33). We know that Piranesi was aided in 1760 by the decision of the Conservatori of Rome to repair the three surviving columns of this temple, which were thought to be in danger of collapse. For this purpose scaffolding was, unusually, erected, of which Piranesi was quick to take advantage.

As built in its third and last form at the start of the first century, the Temple of Castor and Pollux gave the principal western half of the Forum its final shape, in which all four sides had marble-clad buildings, with only the Temple of Vespasian (AD 79–87) and Arch of Septimius Severus (AD 203) to be added. The Greek cult of Castor and Pollux was introduced to Rome in the fifth century BC and the first of the three temples to them on this site is supposed to have been dedicated in 484 BC. This makes it one of the earliest temples in the Forum, about forty years older than the Parthenon in

Athens. It commemorated the occasion fifteen years earlier when Castor and his twin brother, Pollux, legendary gods, beautiful young men and cavalry heroes announced, after watering their horses at the Lacus Juturnae (Pool of Juturna) in the Forum, an imminent victory for the Romans against the Latins.

This victory duly occurred at Lake Regillus, fourteen miles from Rome, where the Latins were led by the tyrant Tarquinius Superbus. The Temple of Castor and Pollux was thus a striking example of a building conceived as a memorial to a half-mythic moment, for the Battle of Lake Regillus was a key event for the Romans in the understanding of their distant past, well known from the account of it in Book II of Livy's *Roman History*. The twins, who fought in this battle, were commemorated by a ritual order of Roman knights (cavalry officers), forming part of the ceremonial life of the Forum. It is characteristic of the myth-making of the Romans that they appropriated for their own benefit the gods of defeated Greece, for Castor and Pollux were the Greek Dios Kouri, legendary sons of Zeus and Leda.

As rebuilt in 117 BC, the temple was hailed by Cicero about fifty years later as 'that famous and noble monument, a temple placed where the eyes of the Roman people see it every day, where the Senate often meets, which is daily thronged by those who come to consult on the gravest issues'. One of the most important temples in the Forum, it characteristically served many purposes. The pronaos (interior) of its spacious portico, eight columns wide and three deep, provided a speakers' platform for political meetings, which included many fierce debates in the late Republic. It was also a setting for the rituals of the Roman knights, while the vaulted spaces of the podium housed, by contrast, the office of weights and measures, as well as safe-deposits or banks for private citizens. Juvenal, who bitterly satirised life under Trajan and Hadrian, observed ironically that 'the most agreeable of pleasures', more entertaining than many theatrical shows, 'was to observe at what risk to life men possess themselves of full treasure-chests bound with brass, or cash that has to be deposited in the guarded Temple of Castor'. Other interiors in the podium had different purposes, including the first taberna (booth or shop) on the west side, which seems from finds discovered in it to have been a combined dentist's premises and beauty parlour.

By the time of Juvenal, the importance of the temple had led to its third and final rebuilding by the future emperor Tiberius, between 7 BC and AD 6, as part of the rebuilding of the Forum planned by Augustus. Its three surviving Carrara marble columns, forty-seven feet high with their entablature, have been regarded for centuries as among the finest examples of the Corinthian order in the ancient world. The two central volutes, or helices, below the abacus of the capitals are unusually intertwined. Since this feature might suggest two people linking their little fingers, it has been interpreted, doubtless fancifully, as symbolising the undying loyalty of the two brothers to each other. It was certainly imitated in the Corinthian columns of the Temple of Castor and Pollux in Naples, which were incorporated into the church of S. Paolo Maggiore formed within the temple. The temple of Castor and Pollux in the Forum is particularly baffling to the modern visitor for there is no means of access to what survives of its high portico, while the archaeological process has exposed the high arches within the podium, which were never meant to be seen.

In the middle of the Forum, near the temple, Piranesi shows the ancient Roman granite basin set up here in 1593 when a well-head with a segmental pediment was added to it. It served as a welcome drinking fountain until the basin was unfortunately removed by Pius VII in 1818 to the Piazza del Quirinale, in front of his summer residence, the Quirinal Palace. Here, it was sunk into the ground so that carters could drive their teams of horses through it to refresh them.

### COLUMN OF PHOCAS

Piranesi's view of the whole length of the Forum from west to east (fig. 1) includes in the foreground three monuments near its western end: the Column of Phocas, the Temple of Vespasian and the Temple of Saturn. The Column of Phocas is the single, free-standing column that we can see isolated between two tall, now long-demolished houses. The singular interest of this still-surviving Corinthian column is that the Byzantine Governor of Italy surmounted it with a statue of Byzantine Emperor Phocas in AD 608, thus forming the last ancient momument added to the Forum. Included in another view by Piranesi (fig. 6), it was originally approached up an imposing pyramidal flight of steps, buried in Piranesi's day, the excavation of which we shall investigate in Chapter 6.

This column of white Proconnesian marble, possibly dating from the second century AD, had been moved to this site in the late third or early fourth century AD, partly to serve as a landmark or sightline. Phocas has recently been described as 'a brutal centurion in the Byzantine army who had usurped the throne in 602 by assassinating the emperor Maurice and his five sons'. However, he is indirectly responsible for

14. *Temple of Vespasian before excavation (Piranesi,* Vedute di Roma, c. *1748–78).* Piranesi captures one of the more bizarre aspects of the Forum in its role as the Campo Vaccino where the piles of earth and rubbish at the west end reached almost to the top of the columns of the Temple of Vespasian. In Piranesi's day this was identified as the Temple of Jupiter Tonans.

preserving the Pantheon, since he gave it to Pope Boniface IV in 608 for use as a church, making it the first temple in Rome to be Christianised. Like other commemorative columns in the Forum, the Column of Phocas loses most of its effect without the gilded statue which crowned it. This should surely be replaced with a copy, which would be in accordance with ancient Roman practice in which many, though far from all, statues were copies of Greek ones.

## TEMPLE OF VESPASIAN

Below the Column of Phocas, Piranesi shows to its right the fragmentary survival of the Temple of Vespasian, which he identified as that of Jupiter the Thunderer, as Palladio had before him (fig. 1). Three of its columns of white Italian marble, forty feet high, and the sections of entablature which they support, are all that survive of this temple, but Piranesi could only show the top of the columns and the capitals, for they were almost completely buried in his day (fig. 14). As with the Column of Phocas, we shall give the extraordinary tale of its eventual excavation in Chapter 6.

The temple was begun on a sloping site below the Tabularium on the death of the Emperor Vespasian in AD 79 by his sons, Titus and Domitian. When Titus himself died two years later, his successor as emperor, Domitian, continued it, adding the name of Titus to its dedication in AD 87. Suetonius tell us that Vespasian, finding the sight of collapsed buildings following fires unsightly, was a great builder. He was responsible for the vast Temple of Peace on the north side of the Forum and, nearby, the Colosseum, a monument of public entertainment which he built on the site of Nero's private

15. *Temple of Vespasian, frieze (in the Tabularium Museum).* Part of the frieze also survives in situ on the temple. It is unusually carved with bold images of the instruments used in animal sacrifices.

lake so as to stress his own beneficence in contrast to Nero's self-indulgence. The first emperor after Augustus and Claudius to be deified, Vespasian is supposed to have announced his imminent death with the lament, 'Pity, I think I'm turning into a God.'

The Temple of Vespasian has recently been described as 'one of the highest achievements of imperial Rome, representing a level of refinement and grace that exceeded that of the Augustan period'. This is due in great part to the delicacy and refinement of the carving, especially of the Corinthian capitals. Caesar and Augustus, who had introduced Carrara marble to Roman buildings, found that the Greek craftsmen in Rome could work this material more skilfully than any native carvers. It was to the growth of such craftsmanship that work like that at the Temple of Vespasian was indebted.

The entablature on the front of the temple was covered with a large inscription, of which the only surviving portion reads RESTITVER, part of *restituerunt* ('they restored'). This refers to the activities at the temple of the emperor Septimius Severus and his son, emperor Caracalla (reigned AD 211–17), though it must be confessed that it is not clear exactly what part of this building they restored. Especially striking is the bold and highly inventive frieze in the entablature, which features images of sacrifice, bull's skulls, a knife, an axe, a plate, a jug and a helmet, referring to the ceremonial role of the emperor as Pontifex Maximus. This can be seen on the short north return of the entablature, of which some elements have been removed to the museum in the Tabularium. Because of the partial burial of the temple in the time of Piranesi, this dramatic frieze was then almost at eye level, an effect which he chose to record in separate engravings.

In our clockwise tour of Piranesi's engraving of the Forum from the Palazzo Senatorio (fig. 1), which we began with the Arch of Septimius Severus, we now reach the last, the Temple of Saturn, identified in his day as that of Concord. Since he could only manage to fit in just two of its eight surviving columns on the extreme right of his engraving, he prepared another fuller view of it (fig. 16), which is one of the most striking of his images of the Forum. In this, he shows the temple incorporating a house with a rather delectable roof terrace sporting potted plants below a pergola, and a line of washing strung between its columns. It was in those days linked to a long street of shops and houses, which he shows terminated by the apse of S. Maria della Consolazione, built in 1583–1600 in the restrained Roman Mannerist style by the papal architect Martino Longhi the Elder. Though the street has gone, the church survives, its apse still visible from this point, so the visitor can appropriately explore it when visiting the Forum.

Occupying one of the oldest sacred sites in the Forum after the Temple of Vesta, this temple is believed to have been founded around the end of the sixth century BC, in the last years of the monarchy or in the early Republic. It was thus the earliest of the Etrusco-Roman temples in the Forum, but it was several times rebuilt, notably in *c.* 42 BC. Saturn was traditionally an ancient king of Rome and also the god of sowing and of corn who founded a golden age in which he introduced agriculture. His name has sometimes been supposed to derive from the Latin word *satum* ('sown'). Virgil looked back to him with reverence, for agriculture was always the basis of the economy of Rome. Saturn is familiar in the

16. *Temple of Saturn (Piranesi,* Vedute di Roma, *c. 1748–78).* In this vivid
image of the invasion of the Forum by animal life and domestic architecture
the buildings in the now vanished street lead up to the still surviving church
of Sta Maria della Consolazione.

Christian church as the origin of the festival of Christmas, the seven days of Saturnalia when gifts were exchanged.

The eight surviving columns of the Temple of Saturn belong to its complete rebuilding at a late but uncertain date in the fourth century AD. This is so late that the temple has been seen almost as a kind of pagan revivalism in the Christian era, for the temples were supposed to have been closed in 356, though the law prescribing this was not very rigorously imposed. The columns of Egyptian granite, thirty-six feet high, were salvaged from earlier structures on different sites, but their richly decorated Ionic capitals were newly made in white marble. The frieze of lacy ornamental carving that can be seen on the south-facing rear of the main architrave was probably part of the rebuilt temple of *c.* 42 BC.

On the architrave over the north entrance front is an inscription, partly shown by Piranesi, which reads in full, SENATUS POPULUSQUE ROMANUS INCENDIO CONSUMPTUM RESTITUIT ('Destroyed by fire, restored by the Senate and People of Rome'). The way in which religion interlocked with every aspect of life in the Roman state was demonstrated by the fact that this temple housed the state treasury, probably in a strong room in the high podium.

In the absence of any surviving flights of steps, it is difficult to reconstruct in one's mind how access was gained to the Temple of Saturn, towering above its giant podium. It is also a matter of puzzlement how, at triumphal processions to the Temple of Jupiter Capitolinus, the chariots containing the emperor, generals and massive amounts of heavy loot could have passed safely up the immensely steep incline of the Clivus Capitolinus, which partly survives at the side of the Temple of Saturn. Indeed, Suetonius tells us that Julius

Caesar was all but thrown to the ground when the axle of his chariot broke elsewhere in Rome on the first of his four processions in the city. He performed an improbable act of atonement by climbing up the stairs to the Capitol by torchlight, accompanied by elephants, and, according to Dio Cassius in his *Roman History*, on his knees.

Piranesi's views of the Forum, a place he knew and loved as an architect, artist and archaeologist, form perhaps the most captivating record of any part of a historic city. However, it is now time that we turned to those monuments in the Forum that, for reasons we shall explain, Piranesi could not record.

# 3

WHAT PIRANESI DOES NOT SHOW

In the last chapter we visited the ancient buildings of the Forum as they had survived until the eighteenth century. We did so with the help of Piranesi because his powerful engravings stimulate our imagination and at the same time bear the stamp of authenticity, having been made before two centuries of excavation exposed long-buried fragments of further buildings, some of which have been subjected to an elaborate process of reconstitution. Any building Piranesi could not see was obviously not the kind of major substantial construction that we saw in the last chapter. Thus, what we will investigate here will be either the fairly unimpressive traces of once-great buildings, or buildings that have been rebuilt, for, as we have pointed out, some of the favourite monuments of today's visitors are in fact modern, though they may look ancient. Moreover, even here in the centre of the Roman world, we still do not know what a fair number of the buildings were actually for.

When Augustus carried out his complete makeover of the Forum around the beginning of the first century AD, he evidently sought to provide his subjects not only with pomp but also with smaller objects of history, religion and romance, with which they could more easily identify. Some of these monuments were bizarre, even semi-nonsensical, and were preserved only on Augustus' whim. They were not excavated before the late nineteenth century so were unknown to Piranesi; they are still easily missed by the visitor to whom they are mostly fairly impenetrable. The principal ones are the Shrine of Juturna, near the Temple of Castor and Pollux, the Lake of Curtius, near the Basilica Julia, the Black Stone, in front of the Senate House, and the Shrine of Venus Cloacina, near the Basilica Aemilia.

Though archaeologists have dug many holes in the Forum to expose the sites of early shrines, this chapter will not concentrate on those but on the remains of substantial structures of the Republic and empire. Beginning at the west end of the Forum, we shall follow roughly the clockwise route taken in the last chapter, dealing with the monuments in groups. We will explain their significance in the life of the Forum in antiquity, while the story of their excavation will be given in subsequent chapters on the Forum from the post-antique world to the present day.

### TABULARIUM, TEMPLE OF CONCORD AND PORTICO OF THE HARMONIOUS GODS

These monuments, each unrecorded by Piranesi for a different reason, illustrate three of the contrasting themes in this book: the Tabularium had survived from antiquity but was largely concealed in Piranesi's day, though he would have been thrilled with it if he had seen it after its uncovering by archaeologists (fig. 17); the Temple of Concord (fig. 17) is a major monument of which virtually nothing survives; and the Portico of the Dei Consentes (Harmonious Gods) is essentially a modern fabrication (fig. 18).

17. *The Tabularium with the Temples of Vespasian and of Concord (reconstruction by Constant Moyaux, 1866).* On the extreme left can just be seen the Temple of Saturn, showing how these three temples were jammed together below the Tabularium, the record office of the Republican period. At the foot of the steps is the altar on which the sacrifices took place. On the right is the Arch of Septimius Severus.

Piranesi did not record the cliff-like building now known as the Tabularium, because its massive arches and arcades had either been concealed behind a stucco facing incorporating windows in the Middle Ages and Renaissance or been buried in accumulated earth. It was gradually unpicked and exposed during the first half of the nineteenth century, while the two arcades were not re-opened until 1939. The most substantial of any surviving building of Republican date in Rome, it is believed to have been in part the state record office, though probably not one in our terms, while there is some disagreement about how it worked. The name Tabularium has been given to it because it housed records inscribed on bronze tablets.

Part of the reconstruction of the Capitoline Hill by the dictator Sulla (reigned 81–79 BC), the Tabularium provided a monumental backdrop to the Forum beneath it. It is also a masterly response to its challenging site, for some of its vaulted rooms had to be cut into the rock of the hill. The façade was also an early example of what became a Roman technique in which, as at the Colosseum, tiers of arches were decorated with ornamental columns, the weight being carried at the Tabularium by the giant piers between the arches. It bears two inscriptions, one now lost, from which it has been supposed that it was completed and dedicated by the consul in 78 BC, Lutatius Catulus, with Lucius Cornelius, a Roman citizen about whom nothing else is known, as architect.

What we see from the Forum today is divided into three parts: the lower section with its giant arches is ancient Roman; above this is the rather featureless but many-windowed, three-storeyed façade built in the medieval and Renaissance periods as the back of the Palazzo Senatorio on the Capitoline Hill;

finally, the whole building is crowned in the centre by a tall campanile with two tiers of arches, built in 1578 by Martino Longhi the Elder, papal architect to Pope Gregory XIII, to replace a medieval tower. The main three-storeyed façade has nothing of the interest of that which Michelangelo built on the other side of the building facing the Capitoline Hill. This is partly because views in and from the Forum were not widely considered of importance in the sixteenth century.

The newly restored interiors of the Tabularium include a long, vaulted gallery of immensely high unmoulded arches that recalls the *Carceri* engravings of the 1740s by Piranesi depicting sinister prisons. These imaginative, even fantastic, images show how far Piranesi had caught the spatial excitement of which Republican architects were capable. From this dramatic space we have a superb view of the Forum with the Alban Hills visible in the far distance.

Immediately below the Tabularium stood the Temple of Concord (Concordia Augusta, or Harmony in the Imperial Family). Probably of the mid fourth century BC in origin, the Temple of Concord was restored in 121 BC, from which time dates the surviving heap of concrete forming part of its base. It was built anew in the reign of Augustus by his heir-apparent, Tiberius, who dedicated it to Concord in AD 10 to celebrate the national unity which it was hoped would follow the concord between members of the imperial family.

Opulent and rich with varied marbles, like the adjacent Temple of Vespasian, the Temple of Concord was one of the most important in the Forum; its destruction during the late middle ages or early Renaissance for the re-use of its materials was a disaster. Because of its long, narrow site it had an unusual plan, with its entrance portico in the centre of one of its long sides. Through windows on either side of the portico one could see fine Greek works of art inside, including marble and bronze sculpture, paintings and smaller objects, for the temple was endowed as a museum by Tiberius, his mother, Livia, and his step-father, Augustus.

Its rather secular, hall-like interior was occasionally used for meetings of the Senate, notably when Cicero delivered his famous speech in 63 BC denouncing the companions of Catiline, who was seen by Roman historians as an evil conspirator in the civil strife of his day. As we shall see in Chapter 4, his fellow conspirators were led directly from the Temple of Concord to be put to death in the Tullianum (Mamertine prison), the only state prison known in ancient Rome, which stood conveniently next to the Temple of Concord.

The sumptuously decorated entablature of the temple helped to establish the classic Corinthian cornice, enriched with modillions, the decorative brackets appearing to support the cornice. A section of this entablature can be seen in the gallery in the Tabularium, while in the Forum Antiquarium, the museum at the other, east, end of the Forum, are displayed column bases and a composite Corinthian capital from the temple, exceptionally featuring vigorous pairs of rams at the angles instead of volutes.

We now pass to the third and last in the group of three monuments at the west end of the Forum, the Portico of the Harmonious Gods (fig. 18), which is totally different from the once-imposing Temple of Concord to its south. It is a bizarre little structure which turns out to be almost entirely of nineteenth- and twentieth-century reconstruction, but no less interesting for that. The harmonious gods, the twelve deities who protected Rome, were in origin the Greek Olympian

18. *Portico of the Harmonious Gods, as rebuilt in 1858.* This colonnade of twelve Corinthian columns set below the Tabularium at an awkward obtuse angle, was built in 1858 by Pope Pius IX. Of the seven of its columns in which he incorporated antique elements four can be seen on the left-hand side. It had been rebuilt in AD 367 as the last pagan religious monument in the Forum, after attempts had been made to close down the temples.

gods, six male paired with six female. On the awkward trapezoidal platform, twelve short Corinthian columns form a portico on two sides of an obtuse angle, a uniquely ugly form. The building originally contained eight rooms made of brick with a further seven in the platform below.

According to an inscription on it, it was rebuilt in AD 367 by the City Prefect, Vettius Praetextatus, despite laws passed with the aim of banning sacrifices in 341 and of closing temples in 356. A learned and obstinate pagan under the conciliatory Emperor Valentinian I (reigned 364–75), Praetextatus, sparred with St Jerome and St Damasus. His Portico of the Harmonious Gods was, with the rebuilt Temple of Saturn, adjacent on its west, the last pagan religious monument in the Forum.

The surviving fragments, perhaps of Hadrianic date, which were discovered when the site was excavated in 1834 by Pope Gregory XVI, were incorporated into an ambitious recreation of the building in 1858 by Pope Pius IX. As a remarkable tribute from a modern pope to ancient pagans, this must be one of the most historically fascinating monuments in the Forum, though one probably not given much attention by visitors. The seven fluted columns of green marble on the left incorporate antique work, including some elements of the original entablature, while the five unfluted columns of travertine limestone on the right date from 1858. The names and dates of both popes are recorded on contemporary plaques, showing the continuing papal interest in pagan monuments well into the nineteenth century. Further restoration was carried out in the 1960s and in 2000.

This area of the Forum must always have been a total muddle, for jammed together at different levels on a cramped sloping site were the Portico of Harmonious Gods, the

Temples of Concord, Vespasian and Saturn, and the important continuation between them of the Via Sacra, known here as the Clivus Capitolinus (Capitoline slope). The Temples of Concord and Vespasian, though standing side by side, bore no architectural relation to each other, the portico of the latter projecting well in advance of that of the former. It is unclear how all these temples were approached from the Forum and from each other. Indeed, the Temple of Vespasian was so awkwardly placed that it permanently blocked the entrance to the staircase leading out of the Tabularium.

## BASILICA AEMILIA AND TEMPLE OF DIVUS JULIUS

The north side of the Forum, between the surviving Senate House and Temple of Antoninus and Faustina, was comprised of the enormous Basilica Aemilia, with the Temple of Divus Julius at right angles to it at its east end. Both this temple and the Basilica Aemilia were buildings of vast ancient repute and historical significance, yet they were almost entirely destroyed centuries ago. Timber-roofed buildings such as the Basilica Aemilia were always a fire hazard. Indeed, it was gutted in the great fire in AD 410 during the sack of Rome by Alaric the Visigoth, while further damage was caused by the earthquake of AD 847. Its surviving fragments were finally dismantled for re-use as building materials in the Renaissance. Nonetheless, it has recently been described by the leading archaeologist Filippo Coarelli as 'the only surviving Republican basilica', the statement of a professional which will disappoint the visitor on discovering that nothing very significant now survives of it apart from its floor, on which sections of columns are lined up horizontally side by side. About as attractive as the site of a mass grave, the area is now closed to the public. Visitors can no longer even enjoy searching the marble paving for the green stains that, improbably, are traditionally said to be of bronze coins that melted into it when they were left behind by terrified money-lenders fleeing the sack of Alaric. The vast but largely empty space created by archaeologists from the nineteenth century onwards gives an impression of the Forum even more misleading than the houses that occupied the site of the Basilica Aemilia when Piranesi made his engravings.

The basilica, though derived as a building type from the cities of the Hellenistic east, was reconstructed by the Romans in the late third or second century BC, as a large covered space providing shelter for a variety of activities, notably law, commerce and business, including, in the Basilica Aemilia, money-changing by the shopkeepers who occupied premises between it and the Forum. The earliest basilica on this site, the Basilica Fulvia, was built in 179 BC but was replaced more than once, for the first time in 55–34 BC by the Basilica Aemilia. This was destroyed by fire in 14 BC and replaced in 2 BC by a lavish building paid for by Augustus. The shops were aggrandised into an imposing two-storeyed frontage known as the New Shops, though the official name was the Porticus of Caius and Lucius Caesar, grandsons and chosen successors of Augustus. They predeceased him and in their honour he built a chapel beside it.

The Porticus of Caius and Lucius Caesar, a grandiose version of the stoas in Hellenistic towns, entirely concealed the basilica, which was a rectangular hall, very narrow for its considerable length and lit by a simple clerestorey. After further enrichments with marble columns in AD 22, the porticus became one of the most admired buildings in Rome and beyond. Indeed, this two-storeyed building with open round-headed arcades on three sides was soon described by Pliny the Elder as one of the three 'most beautiful the world has ever seen', together with the Temple of Peace and the Forum of Augustus in Rome. We can see what he meant from looking at a drawing by Giuliano da San Gallo of *c.* 1500 of the elaborately inventive Doric north return elevation of the porticus, which shows rich decorative detail such as the rosettes in the necking bands of its capitals (fig. 19). Also, a section of a vigorously carved frieze of the late first century BC, including scenes from the legendary history of Rome, survives in the Forum Antiquarium. Here, too, can be seen figures of Phrygian barbarian caryatids from the basilica.

Pliny's interest in buildings was primarily in making lists of the stones used in them; when he observed that, 'among our truly noble buildings', the Basilica of Aemilia is 'remarkable for its columns from Phrygia', he was referring to the white marble columns with crimson or purple markings, brought from Synnada in Phrygia, the modern Turkey. An unbelievably prolific author as well as a soldier, lawyer and treasury officer in provinces throughout the Empire, Pliny was well aware that to erect public buildings and subsidise public leisure were important ways in which an emperor could elicit popular support. Seeing the basilica, the nearby Forum of Augustus, and the Temple of Peace as expressing the magnanimity of emperors and of the power of the Roman Empire, Pliny claimed that to 'review the resources derived from the experiences of eight hundred years' will 'show that here too in our buildings we have vanquished the world'. Ironically, despite believing that Rome had 'vanquished the

19. *The Porticus of Caius and Lucius Caesar at the Basilica Aemilia (drawn by Giuliano da San Gallo, c. 1500)*. Built by Augustus in 2 BC, the Basilica Aemilia was described by Pliny the Elder as 'one of the most beautiful the world has ever seen'. We are indebted to the architect San Gallo for this unique record of a now lost but sumptuously carved marble building which featured, unusually, rosettes in the capitals of its Doric columns.

world', Pliny himself perished in the great eruption of Vesuvius that destroyed the cities of Pompeii and Herculaneum.

In the end, it is very difficult for us to envisage how lively or attractive the great basilicas in the Forum were in real life, or to imagine what went on in their upper storeys. What we surely can do is see the Basilica Aemilia and the Basilica Julia opposite it as manifestations of the imperial will to build and of a desire to define grandiosely the north and south sides of the Forum. The idea that the Forum was a planned piazza as far back as the second and first centuries BC must be rejected; the east side of the space was not defined until the building in 29 BC of the Temple of Divus Julius, which we shall consider now.

The Temple of Divus Julius ('Deified Julius [Caesar]'), the dictator who was turned into a god two years after his assassination, was hugely significant both as a structure and in its location: it was built on the spot to which, after his funeral in the Forum, Julius Caesar was brought by the public after the Ides of March for cremation in front of the Regia, the office which he had used as Pontifex Maximus. The temple to his memory, probably the first in Rome dedicated to an ex-mortal, was built on this site by his great nephew, Augustus.

Remarkably for a building so central to the history of Rome and the Forum, the marble foundations and stone walls of the Temple of Divus Julius were reduced to lime in the mid sixteenth century for the building of St Peter's, under Pope Paul III. Nothing now survives of it except for the rubble core of its base, though there is an ugly rebuilt section of the brown tufa and concrete wall of the platform in front of it. The semicircular recess in the centre of this platform shelters a lump of decayed stone, possibly the remains of a circular altar replacing the one where Caesar's body was burnt before the temple was built. This recess has recently been protected by a little wooden roof to which visitors are drawn with its suggestion that they will find beneath it something of special interest. Some of them accordingly leave bunches of flowers wrapped in cellophane at this site. It was on this platform that the body of Augustus lay in state in AD 14 and where his stepson and heir, Tiberius, gave his funeral oration. Behind and to the south of the temple, and also unknown to Piranesi, was the Temple of Vesta.

## TEMPLE OF VESTA AND
## HOUSE OF THE VESTAL VIRGINS

Visitors to the Forum will probably have heard more about the Vestal Virgins than any other aspect of Roman religion – not inappropriately, since by the late Republic the Virgins were the only people living in the Forum. This was to enable them to perform their enormously important task of keeping the fire in the Temple of Vesta continually burning, thereby maintaining the perpetuity of the Roman state. However, of the once-imposing House of the Vestal Virgins virtually nothing survives, while the Temple of Vesta is, rather surprisingly, a twentieth-century re-creation (fig. 20). Of this circular temple what we see today is a section of its colonnade rebuilt in 1933 by Alfonso Bartoli, following a suggestion of Giacomo Boni, who directed excavations in the Forum from 1899 to 1925. Since so little of it had survived, its reconstructed appearance was derived from small images on coins and a first-century AD relief in the Uffizi in Florence that possibly depicts it. Yet, as we saw in the Introduction, despite its twentieth-century form, the Temple of Vesta was given pride

20. *Temple of Vesta, as reconstructed in 1933.* This twentieth-century building incorporates some fragments of the temple in its final form as restored in *c.* 200 AD by the wife of the emperor, Septimius Severus. It was ringed by twenty Corinthian columns standing on a tall podium.

of place on the cover of Amanda Claridge's invaluable *Rome: An Oxford Archaeological Guide*.

Vesta was adapted by the Romans from the Greek goddess Hestia, the daughter of Saturn and virgin goddess of the hearth and home, who lived on Mount Olympus. In Rome, she was served by priestesses, or Vestals, who also had to remain virgins. This was a tradition familiar in ancient Greece, with its ever-burning fires in temples and city centres acting as a focus for social, political and religious activity. As Mary Beard has recently explained, the significance of Vesta's hearth lay in 'its link with the foundation, generation and continuation of the race. The goddess Vesta encapsulated all these elements; she was the flame itself, she was the virgin, she was Vesta the mother.'

It has been claimed that the preservation of a vestal flame was a custom in the houses of some ordinary Roman citizens, while a parallel convention is retained today in Roman Catholic churches where the sanctuary lamp before the Blessed Sacrament in the tabernacle is never allowed to go out. The Vestals were entrusted with the keeping of iconic objects such as the Palladium, a statue of Athena supposedly brought to Rome from Troy by Aeneas, who had also traditionally brought from Troy the vestal flame. According to the elder Pliny, the Vestals also kept a phallus in their temple. The sacred objects in their care were seen only by them and the Pontifex Maximus. Vesta herself remained a mysterious figure, of whom there was no cult image in her temple during the Republic and early Empire. There have, indeed, been few representations of her in ancient or modern art.

The circular shape and small size of the Temple of Vesta are also of significance and certainly intrigued the ancient

Romans themselves, for they were aware that it looked back to the earliest period of their history. The supposed relation of the temple to the thatched hut of reeds on the Palatine in which Romulus and Remus were brought up by the shepherd Faustulus was recorded by Ovid in Book VI of his *Fasti*. This Iron Age hut was associated with a replica on the Palatine which is said to have survived, many times restored, until the fourth century AD. The cult of Vesta supposedly went back to her first temple on this site in the Forum, probably also of timber and reed, which the Romans attributed to Numa Pompilius. Even after it was rebuilt in stone, it had on several occasions to be replaced after being destroyed by fires, not surprisingly caused by the sacred flames within. In its final form, dating from a restoration of c. AD 200 by Julia Domna, wife of Septimius Severus, it was a circle of twenty Corinthian columns, the frieze carved with images of sacrificial instruments. Smoke could always be seen issuing reassuringly from an opening at the top of the conical bronze roof (fig. 21).

The Vestals, of whom there were only six at any one time, were appointed between the ages of six and ten by the Pontifex Maximus and served for thirty years. In heavy archaic dress and hairstyles, they conducted many elaborate and arcane rituals, such as baking salt for sacred cakes in primitive earthenware and annually throwing straw puppets, representing men bound hand and foot, into the Tiber. If the Temple caught fire, the flames could not be extinguished by water from an ordinary source but only from a sacred spring at the Porta Capena, from which a Vestal drew water every day. This she had to carry back on her head in special jar, which she could not set down on the ground because it would thereby lose all its virtue.

21. *Temple of Vesta, reconstruction in engraving.* Originally built of timber in
the eighth century BC, this temple was circular and modest in size like the
thatched Iron Age huts on the Palatine in which Romulus and Remus were
supposed to have been brought up earlier in the century. It was believed that
the survival of the Roman state would be threatened if the Vestal Virgins
allowed the sacred fire within the temple to go out. The smoke is here shown
emerging reassuringly from an opening in the conical roof of bronze tiles.

Any Vestal who allowed the fire in the Temple of Vesta to go out was flogged unless, like Aemilia and Tuccia, she could perform a miracle such as igniting the dead embers by throwing a cloth on them. If a Vestal had sexual relations with a man, she was buried alive and he was flogged to death by a slave. Livy described the trial for incest in 420 BC of Postumia, who had aroused suspicion with her sense of humour and pretty clothes. Though found not guilty, she was ordered by the Chief Priest 'to stop making jokes and, in her dress and appearance, to aim at looking holy rather than smart'.

The Christian emperor Theodosius the Great (reigned AD 379–95) was tolerant of pagan practices until 391, when he ended the blood sacrifices in the temples on which the security of the state had depended for a thousand years. The law passed in 356 to close the temples had not been fully observed, as we noted earlier. Theodosius caused the flame in the Temple of Vesta to be extinguished finally in 391, telling the Vestal Virgins that their virginity was no long required. 'No one is to go to the sanctuaries,' he declared, 'walk through the temples or raise his eyes to statues created by the labour of man.' It was he who also cancelled the last Olympic Games in 393. Despite its rich religious and historical associations, the Temple of Vesta was itself destroyed in the mid sixteenth century so that its marble blocks could be re-used or burnt for lime. Fragments of it were discovered in excavations between 1877 and 1901, and in 1933, as mentioned above, a section of the colonnade was rebuilt, with much new travertine. On the podium stand three Corinthian columns supporting a full entablature, with their corresponding pilasters on the rusticated wall behind.

After such a reconstruction, it is perhaps not surprising

that the few surviving remains of the nearby House of the Vestal Virgins were also given a makeover in an understandable attempt to make such an important place attractive to visitors. Statues from the second to fourth centuries AD of Head Vestals were placed on tall pedestals around rectangular pools, giving it something of the flavour of a tasteful Edwardian millionaire's garden. Not excavated until the 1880s, this was where the Vestal Virgins led their enclosed life, akin to that of nuns in some of the stricter orders in the Catholic Church. Since it was primarily residential in function, its final form, completed in AD 113 to replace an earlier building, drew on the precedent of private houses with a central garden court or peristyle surrounded by colonnades and containing a rainwater tank. With its large pools, the court in the House of the Vestal Virgins was flanked by two-storeyed colonnades with columns of Carystian green marble below and of variegated red and white limestone above.

If this sumptuous building be thought over-large for six unmarried ladies, we should recall that it was a way of expressing their enormous importance to the preservation of the Roman State, and also that they lived luxuriously, with many servants and slaves. There was a bathing suite, and each enjoyed her own apartment, including rooms with underfloor heating. When a Vestal Virgin went out, her carriage even had right of way in the streets, while if she happened to come across anyone being led to execution she could pardon him.

The Temple of Vesta and the House of the Vestal Virgins formed a complex known as the Atrium Vestae, which was close physically and functionally to the Regia, or 'Royal House', on the north side of the Temple. Housing the cults connected with the person of the king, this building is where the Pontifex Maximus held official meetings, but only fragments of it remain on its wedge-shaped site. Also characteristic of the somewhat incongruous contrasts in the Forum, the back or east side of the House of Vestal Virgins abutted on to utilitarian buildings, probably storehouses, known as the Horrea Vespasiani. Like the House of the Vestal Virgins, these border the Via Nova (New Way) which, despite its name, was an ancient street, running east towards the Arch of Titus.

In the chaos of current excavations, which are exposing a mass of foundations that are not open to the public at the time of writing, it is impossible to reconstruct in one's mind, as elsewhere in the Forum, the network of streets which passed through this area. In another complication, modern excavations have also shown that the Horrea Vespasiani were built over Etruscan and Republican aristocratic houses on the slopes below the Palatine. These were developed from the late sixth century BC, partially on the site of the so-called Wall of Romulus, dating from two centuries earlier.

### SHRINE OF JUTURNA, DOMITIANIC HALL AND PALATINE RAMP

Returning now to the western half of the Forum, we come across monuments which touch on key themes for us, such as the unexpected modern re-creation of certain minor ancient monuments and the unclear function of many major ones, as well as the new topic of the way in which the Forum was watched from on high by the imperial autocracy on the Palatine, at least from the first century. The first of these

22. *Shrine of Juturna, as reconstructed in 1953–5.* This white marble aedicule, flanked by two fluted Corinthian columns, is a twentieth-century building which incorporates a few excavated fragments of the shrine for a statue of Juturna, built in the late third century AD. Nearby is the pool of Juturna, goddess of healing waters, where Castor and Pollux were supposed to have watered their horses after the battle of Lake Regillus.

monuments lies between the House of the Vestal Virgins and the Temple of Castor and Pollux and is one of the more striking of the smaller monuments in the Forum. The Shrine of Juturna, though, like the Temple of Vesta, looks attractive because it is not an ancient ruin but a modern re-construction (fig. 22).

Who was Juturna? She was the goddess of healing waters, whose nearby pool, a square, marble-lined basin of which irregular sections survive, marks the spot where Castor and Pollux are supposed to have watered their horses after the battle of Lake Regillus. About thirty feet to the east of the Pool of Juturna, her shrine is an aedicule sheltering her statue. It is a modest but elegant pedimented structure of white marble supported on two Corinthian columns. Originally built in AD 283, but retaining elements of its predecessor, virtually nothing of the Shrine of Juturna remained in position until 1953–5, when it was entirely rebuilt by the architect A. Davico, incorporating some excavated fragments. It was a curiously insignificant monument on which to lavish so much attention, but it was rebuilt in accordance with the wishes of an American benefactor. Moreover, in 1999 it was awkwardly incorporated into the north wall of the ponderous building erected in that year to cover the frescoes of the Forty Martyrs. Remains survive nearby of rooms that were built, it has inventively been claimed, for visitors who came to take the healing waters. Less romantically, some have suggested that the area became the seat of the water administration of the city.

We find behind the Temple of Castor and Pollux the so-called Domitianic Hall. Though it is a huge building, it was largely engulfed by houses in Piranesi's day, so it hardly shows in his views of the Forum. It reminds us that the Forum is full of baffling mysteries, for, despite its size, little is said about the Domitianic Hall in most guidebooks, because of its uncertain function. This does not prevent archaeologists from making numerous guesses: for example, it has recently been claimed as a priestly college maintaining the cult of Divus Augustus, while before that it was often identified as the nearby Temple of Augustus. Because it is near the site of a cult dedicated to Minerva, it has been hailed as Hadrian's Athenaeum, the niches being book recesses. Other suggestions range from a horreum (storeroom), which seems unlikely for a building almost on the scale of a Norman castle, to a mount for a statue of Augustus. It is anyone's guess.

It was probably begun by the increasingly tyrannical and absolutist emperor Domitian in the early 90s AD. His grandiose plan was to develop this whole corner of the Forum with buildings rising up to the level of the Palatine Hill, where he had built a vast and architecturally fantastic palace for himself. Indeed, near the Domitianic Hall is a covered ramp up to the Palatine, a giant vaulted passage way which is also associated with the building works of Domitian. With its high, arched ceiling, the Palatine Ramp has a Piranesian magic and drama which make it one of the most remarkable sights in the Forum; but it is not shown to the public. This dark and twisting ascent, perhaps originally with guards at every corner, gives one a sense of the fear and policing associated with access to the seat of power in the Empire.

The Palatine Hill to which the ramp leads is another of the many mysteries that confront the visitor. Hanging over the Forum along its southern edge, it is a vast and deeply confusing area of ruins, clumps of trees and gardens, with an unclear relation to the buildings below. Nonetheless, its elite housing overlooked the Forum in the Republican period, while the first emperors made it their base, turning the Palatine into the Palace. Occupying a site larger than either the Forum or the Colosseum, the emperor's palace was vitally important as the seat of the Roman imperial court. This fact is often overlooked, as Andrew Wallace-Hadrill has shown: the court has been dismissed by many historians since it is not mentioned in Roman law, while 'modern liberalism and ancient republicanism combined to ignore it'. Conversely, he stresses that, 'without the court, the Roman state is incomprehensible, for it was the true site of the concentration and redistribution of power.'

### BASILICA JULIA AND THE ROSTRA

Just to the north-west of the Domitianic Hall is, or was, the enormous Basilica Julia, or law courts. Like the Basilica Aemilia, it was also not excavated until long after the time of Piranesi, who was therefore unable to record it. However, as with the Basilica Aemilia, the 'excavation' of the Basilica Julia has exposed nothing more than its floor, so the resultant blankness makes it difficult to envisage the Forum as an enclosed rectangular space. It bordered the Forum on its south side, as the Basilica Aemilia did on the north. Originally as high as the adjacent Temple of Castor and Pollux, the Basilica Julia filled the space between that temple and the Temple of Saturn.

The Basilica Julia replaced the Basilica Sempronia, one of the earliest in Rome, built in 169 BC. Excavations in the 1960s revealed that the Basilica Sempronia had itself been erected on the site of one of the last surviving great houses in the Forum, that of Scipio Africanus (236–183 BC). From an old patrician family, he became the greatest of Roman generals and defeated Hannibal of Carthage. The new Basilica Julia, with a row of shops along its north front, was dedicated in 46 BC by Julius Caesar, from whom it took its name. It was rebuilt more than once, the last time after the fire of AD 283. Cicero famously wrote at this time of 'The Forum in which all justice is preserved', in his Fourth Oration against Catiline, while the younger Pliny recorded trials in which he had pleaded in the Basilica Julia.

In its final form in the late third century, the basilica was surrounded by an open, two-storeyed marble colonnade of arches separated by engaged columns, Doric on the ground floor, Ionic on the first. This was a variant on the Basilica Aemilia, facing it on the other side of the Forum, but its plan and construction were architecturally more ambitious. The ambulatory surrounding the internal hall on both storeys was two bays deep and had stone vaults resting on rectangular piers, not on columns. Its rear façade, facing away from the Forum, is supposed to have been lined with offices for legal officials, bankers or money-changers.

Once again, it is hard to envisage today how such a building worked. Visitors, now unaccountably denied access to what survives of its stone floor, are reduced to searching for the game boards (which at least are easily visible) that were carved as graffiti on the front steps by idling Romans. The brick piers are largely nineteenth-century restorations: the one on the north side, with its attached pilaster and springing of an arch, is the work of the archaeologist Pietro Rosa, who excavated the foundations of the building in the 1850s.

Along the top of the steps, modern archaeologists have set up various small ancient Roman monuments and inscriptions which, though decorative in themselves, have no meaningful relation to the function of the building. They are not normally explained in guidebooks, which also contain little on what visitors will find visually the most prominent feature of the basilica: the large brick arches in the south-west corner. These date from a restoration by Diocletian, and some scholars believe they were later incorporated into the medieval church of S. Maria in Cannapara, which took its name from the Cannaparia, the rope or cord manufactory established in the outer aisles of the basilica in the late medieval period.

We turn, finally, to what was one of the most important features in the secular life of the Forum. The Rostra, or speaker's platform for public magistrates, was first built around the end of the sixth century BC and is associated with the beginning of the Republic in 509 BC. This became not only a symbol of the Forum as the centre of the government of Rome and eventually of the empire, but also a clear statement of the identity of political and military power. This is because on to the front of the platform from which the orators spoke were fastened the bronze prows or beaks of ships, in reference to those captured when the Romans defeated the Latins in the decisive naval battle of Antium (Anzio) in 338 BC. It was these which gave the Rostra its name, *rostrum* being the word for a ship's prow. We can see on the front wall of the Rostra the dowel holes that were drilled to secure the prows, but it should be pointed out that this platform, ten feet high, eight long and forty deep, is a reconstruction of 1904. It is made up of very small stone fragments, though it incorporates a few original tufa blocks at its north-east corner.

23. *Marble relief of imperial scenes in the Forum (the Anaglypha Traiani), early second century AD (Senate House).* One of two relief panels discovered in the Forum, about which, as with so much in the Forum, there is considerable uncertainty: it is not known whether Trajan or Hadrian is the principal subject; which buildings are depicted; and where the reliefs were originally situated. The emperor performs two imperial acts, the *adlocutio* on the left, a speech made at the Rostra, probably in front of the Temple of Divus Julius, and the *alimentaria* on the right, the distribution of free food, in front of the Basilica Julia.

The Rostra was begun in this form and on this site by Julius Caesar, who chose this new and commanding position for it, facing centrally down the length of the Forum from its western end, as part of his plan of 46 BC for dignifying the Forum. His Rostra, completed after his death by Augustus, replaced a previous Rostra that was nearer the Senate House. With characteristic Roman piety, the new building echoed the old one in its concave rear. It is assumed that it was at the Rostra that Antony delivered his celebrated funeral speech for Julius Caesar. In AD 303 the platform was made considerably more impressive than it is now by being surmounted by a row of five columns crowned by commemorative statues to mark the first visit to Rome of Diocletian. Balancing it at the other end of the Forum, further rostra were built in the late Empire in front of the Temple of Divus Julius, but the remains were destroyed in the nineteenth century by archaeologists in the false belief that they were medieval and therefore of no interest.

Displayed today in the Senate House are two sculptural reliefs, known as the Anaglypha Traiani (AD 117–20). One of these brings the Forum alive for us, since it shows Trajan addressing the people from the Rostra in front of the Temple of Divus Julius, and it possibly also depicts the Basilica Julia, the Temple of Castor and Pollux and the long-destroyed Arch of Augustus (fig. 23).

Having completed our survey of the ancient buildings in the Forum, first with and then without the help of Piranesi, we are ready to turn in the next chapter to what some of the archaeologists and guidebooks do not really want us to consider, the post-antique monuments and life of the Forum.

# 4

## CHURCHES IN THE FORUM

Piranesi's panoramic views of the Forum and its ruinous remains feature six roofed and working buildings, which all turn out to be churches: S. Adriano, built into the Senate House, S. Lorenzo in Miranda, built into the Temple of Antoninus and Faustina, SS. Cosmas and Damian, S. Francesca Romana, SS. Luca e Martina, and the now demolished S. Maria Liberatrice. The Forum had become a Christian sacred space. Indeed, it has been a place of worship for about 2,800 years, and for over half that time the worship has been Christian. The churches were all entered from, and looked on to, the Forum. But the growth of archaeology and the transformation of the space into a designated archaeological site means that those of them that survive now tend to be entered from outside the Forum, in other words from their rear. They have in effect been written out of the Forum's history. This hostility to them goes back to the early days of the archaeological process: for example, in her three-volumed *Rome in the Nineteenth Century* (1820), Charlotte Eaton dismissed S. Lorenzo as 'now shut up, but ought to be pulled down', while Horace Marucchi in *The Roman Forum and the Palatine* (1906) welcomed the recent destruction of S. Maria Liberatrice and called for a similar fate to be meted out to S. Lorenzo.

Nonetheless, the standing buildings that the modern visitor to the Forum sees are still churches, which is a nice echo of the ancient Roman Forum where, it should not be forgotten, the great majority of buildings were religious in function, even if modern accounts of the Forum tend to stress its political significance above all else. These churches contain everything that is to be expected in the historic Catholic churches of Italy: frescoes, mosaics, altar pieces, tombs, monuments, shrines, relics, and objects of veneration such as an ancient Roman stone, preserved in S. Francesca Romana, which supposedly bears the imprint of the knees of St Peter. However, with the huge decline in Mass attendance and in vocations to the priesthood, following the self-destructive reforms of the Second Vatican Council, the prime function of the churches in the Forum is now to provide a colourful setting for weddings. Nonetheless, as we shall see, they are wonderful places to visit, even if they have become difficult to appreciate for a range of reasons, notably their banishment from the Forum of which they were once a part.

Christianity already had a presence in the city when St Peter preached there *c.* AD 60 and St Paul wrote his letter to the Romans from Corinth. By the end of the second century or mid third century, a prosperous Christian community flourished in Rome. The decline of the Roman Empire was associated not so much with the rise of Christianity as with the military anarchy that characterised the third century AD, but emperors often found Christians a convenient scapegoat. Their punishment was a symbol of imperial power as well as a reaffirmation of the traditional, pagan, gods. Among those seeking to restore order was, for example, Diocletian (reigned 284–305), who reorganised the entire empire and was a great builder and a persecutor of Christians. But the new religion's status was transformed on 28 October AD 312 when Constantine, a Christian supporter who was formally baptised on his death bed, wrested the city of Rome from his co-emperor Maxentius. Maxentius had been a significant architectural patron, as was Constantine, who built churches as well as public buildings and completed, as we have seen, the Basilica of Maxentius.

The earliest churches were built on the margins of Rome and thus did not touch the Forum. The great Roman families who dominated the Senate and the centre of the city were still pagan, but Constantine built churches that were in fact mostly memorials to martyrs in Christian cemeteries (this was the origin of St Peter's, among several others). These could only be built over tombs and were therefore outside the main city. In choosing distant sites in the *suburbium*, Constantine helped create the wide spread of the present metropolis and determined its sacred geography – the very earliest large churches being away from the ancient pagan centre of Rome.

The first person to use an ancient Roman building in the Forum as a church was Pope Felix IV (reigned 526–30) when he founded SS. Cosmas and Damian. There had been little call for pagan temples to be turned into Christian churches, partly because they remained imperial property even after the suppression of paganism in 395, so were not immediately available to the church for conversion. In 395 the Roman Empire was split into two halves, both Christian and both with its own emperor. The eastern, or Byzantine, empire, with its capital at Constantinople, survived until the Turks completed their conquest of it in 1453. The short-lived western empire, with its capital first at Milan and then at

Ravenna, was subject to constant barbarian invasion. On its fall in 476, Italy was ruled by the Ostrogoth kings. It was one of these, Theodoric (493–526), another great builder, who made Felix IV pope. Rome had become virtually an outpost of empire by this time, and its population was falling (from a million or a million and a half at the height of the empire to around 90,000 at the end of the sixth century), so it was no longer the vast imperial conurbation it had once been. Yet the Forum still retained real clout. Hence it saw a series of ecclesiastical foundations, modest in some respects and thus in keeping with the smaller scale of the city.

The process of Christianisation was slow. The sixth century saw the creation of just two churches in the Forum, SS. Cosmas and Damian and S. Maria Antiqua. S. Adriano came in the seventh century; the modest SS. Sergio e Bacco had appeared by the late eighth century; S. Maria Nova (now S. Francesca Romana) came in the ninth century; and S. Lorenzo was established by the eleventh century. This is not a particularly impressive list, making it clear that the Forum must still have been dominated by ancient Roman buildings. It was not, however, the kind of depopulated wasteland at this time that it is often supposed to have been. We should note, for example, the stress laid by the Byzantine administration in the mid sixth century on the need for continual upkeep of the Forum; the installation of S. Maria Antiqua at around the same time; the prominent placing of the statue of Phocas in 608; the papal election held in the ancient Comitium before the entire populace in the eighth century; and the mainte-nance of the paving at the original level until at least the sack of Robert Guiscard and his Normans in 1084.

Unlike the early foundations of Constantine in the fourth

century on the periphery of the city, most of the churches founded in Rome in the sixth century up to the time of Gregory the Great (590–604) and the following thirty years were centred on the Forum, the Via Sacra and the Palatine, at the heart of imperial Rome. These were all adaptations of ancient pagan buildings, despite there being some reluctance to take over imperial property. Indeed, Pope Honorius I (reigned 625–38) needed an imperial decree to allow him to take the bronze roof tiles from the Temple of Venus and Roma in the Forum to St Peter's. The same Pope turned the Senate House in the Forum into the church of S. Adriano. It was not until the mid ninth century that a new church, S. Maria Nova, was built from scratch on a site in the Forum. From this point on the city began to disintegrate politically and socially. Between the tenth and thirteenth centuries the impoverished population was reduced to about 35,000, probably dropping to as little as 17,000 during the period from 1309–1377, when the popes and the curia were in Avignon.

## SS. COSMAS AND DAMIAN

The church dedicated in AD 527 to the saints Cosmas and Damian, physicians from Syria who were supposedly martyred under Diocletian, is one of the most fascinating yet challenging monuments in the Forum (fig. 24). It is fascinating because it shows the complexity of the path from paganism to Christianity, being one of the main Christian monuments of the Forum yet occupying a couple of side rooms of the Templum Pacis (Temple of Peace) – a vast complex built between AD 71 and 79 adjacent to, but outside, the Forum itself, to celebrate Roman victory over the Jews ('Temple of Pacification' might thus be a better translation). It was King Theodoric as representative of imperial authority who gave permission for these publicly owned halls to be turned into a church. A further continuity between paganism and Christianity is shown in the fact that the main hall of the Templum Pacis, probably deserted by 520, seems to have served as a medical office in an area which had been settled by doctors in public civil service from the Imperial age onwards. The church thus Christianised an ancient tradition, for, dedicated to two physicians, it was associated with healing and salvation. Like other early churches in the Forum, it also had a special flavour, neither being a parish church nor containing relics. Instead it was one of the *diaconiae*, that is, welfare centres providing food and relief to the poor and to pilgrims. Into this category fell the churches of S. Adriano and S. Maria Antiqua, as well as the little oratory of SS. Sergio e Bacco, which was built against the south side of the Arch of Septimius Severus.

The frequent changes made to SS. Cosmas and Damian, right up to interventions by current archaeologists, pose the problem of how to present a building with such a long history of development. How should we decide to what developmental period or phase it should be restored? Secondly, we now approach the church awkwardly from the modern Via dei Fori Imperiali, through the convent attached to it, rather than as originally from the Via Sacra as it passes through the Forum. The circuitous route begins at the entrance to the convent through the tall, plain arch of white travertine marble which was added in 1947 by the architect Gaetano Rapisardi. Below the prominent bell turret, the left-hand range in ancient brick survives from the Temple of Peace, when it was used to display the Marble Plan of Rome, that remarkable map of the

24. *SS. Cosmas and Damian, apse.* The mid-fourth-century interior of this
church is fascinating as a rare survival of a secular, roofed, ancient Roman
building. Believed to have been the audience hall of the city prefect, it was
used as a church from the early sixth century when the Early Christian
mosaics were introduced into the apse and over the segmental arch
separating it from the body of the building. The decorative work is by Luigi
Arigucci who remodelled the interior in the 1630s, dividing it into almost
two by inserting a new floor.

city inscribed for the Emperor Septimius Severus, which we saw at the start of Chapter 2. We then enter the cloister with arcades on three sides of its ground floor, designed by Luigi Arigucci in the 1630s and frescoed by Francesco Allegrini. We finally enter the church itself, somewhat unexpectedly, from a corner of the cloister.

Nonetheless, it is exciting to visit what is the most intact, roofed survival of part of an ancient Roman building in the Forum. In fact, it comprises two halls from the Temple of Peace, ceded to the pope by the emperor: its nave had probably served as an audience chamber for the city prefect by the early fifth century, while its vestibule or antechapel, a much smaller, domed, circular building, is the so-called 'Temple of Romulus'. We saw this late Roman building, dating from the early fourth century AD, in Chapter 2.

Since Felix IV adapted these two existing buildings, his church is not really an Early Christian building, as it is sometimes described: the apse and upper walls date from the mid fourth century and are thus purely pagan. Indeed, the church echoes the form of the audience halls of late antique rulers, inspired by imperial throne rooms. Felix IV merely added the Early Christian mosaics to the apse and its semi-dome in the 520s, leaving the interior to retain, as it does today, something of the secular flavour of the ancient Roman building, an effect also aided by its great width. However, the sixth-century gold-ground mosaics in the half-dome of the apse are among the earliest and most beautiful in Rome (fig. 24). They include depictions of SS. Peter and Paul introducing SS. Cosmas and Damian, in rich red and violet robes, to Christ, who is in golden draperies and holds a scroll like an ancient Roman orator. St Felix IV, on the extreme left, presents a model of the church, while in a band below these figures are twelve lambs symbolizing the apostles and four rivers symbolizing the gospels. The bold figures and shadows show that the illusionistic traditions of Hellenistic art had not been forgotten by these artists.

Because it does not present a powerful façade to the Forum, the church scarcely shows up in Piranesi's views, but in the 1630s both it and its convent were restored and remodelled by Orazio Torriani and Luigi Arigucci for Pope Urban VIII (reigned 1623–44), a member of the papal family of Barberini and a great architectural patron. Arigucci, who had been appointed Architect of the Papal Camera by Urban VIII in 1630, narrowed the great segmental arch between the nave and apse, created the three chapels on each side of the nave, and made the church two-storeyed by inserting a floor into it because the lower part had become damp through being underground.

This apsed crypt or lower church is now fairly featureless apart from a marble floor with fragments of a thirteenth-century mosaic in the manner of the Cosmati family of Rome. Arigucci continued this floor into the circular 'Temple of Romulus' so that it formed a noble vestibule to the church. The façade to the Forum of the 'Temple of Romulus' was also given at about this time a Baroque flavour, with an attractive cupola and a segmental pediment rising high above the front walls. The pediment was needlessly destroyed in 1879–80, though the cupola was surprisingly retained and survives today. The eighteenth-century Neapolitan *presepe* (crib), recently moved to a domed lobby in one corner of the cloister, was handsomely displayed in this vestibule until around 1990, when the archaeologists destroyed Arrigucci's marble floor. It had been the perfect home for the *presepe*, a huge and elaborate assembly of many fine figures in terracotta, porcelain and wood, depicting the Adoration of the Magi.

One can look into the circular 'Temple of Romulus', now an empty and functionless vestibule, through a wall of glass installed at the end of the nave of SS. Cosmas and Damian in 2000, and one can also enter it from the Forum. But the decorative treatment has been removed from its walls, leaving bare brick, so that it has neither an antique Roman flavour nor a seventeenth-century one. The survival of a well below its floor has led to the suggestion that it may have been associated with the healing arts of the two saints to whom the church is dedicated, an echo of the temple opposite of the twin gods, Castor and Pollux.

The great importance of the two buildings which Felix turned into SS. Cosmas and Damian is their antiquity, for they do not have enormous architectural quality. Indeed, it is understandable that the aim of many visitors to the church is either to be married in it or to admire only the Early Christian mosaics in its apse.

We now turn to other ruined buildings which have been excavated and restored by archaeologists and where similar problems arise.

### S. MARIA ANTIQUA AND ORATORY OF THE FORTY MARTYRS

The church of S. Maria Antiqua, dating from the reign of Justin II (565–78), about fifty years after the foundation of the church of SS. Cosmas and Damian, was the second conversion into a church of an ancient Roman building in the

Forum. This time, it was not a temple that was adapted for Christian use but a square atrium with porticoes near the foot of the Palatine at the back of the Temple of Castor and Pollux. This was part of a complex structure built in the late first century at the side of a great ramp begun by Domitian to lead up to the palaces on the Palatine. It is thus fascinating to see a church being made out of an ancient building whose function was secular, in this case part of the forecourt of an imperial palace. There is also an irony in that the exposure of the remains of S. Maria Antiqua was made possible only by the total demolition by twentieth-century archaeologists of the handsome Renaissance church of S. Maria Liberatrice, which had been built into it.

In the mid sixth century, when Rome was politically in a province of the Byzantine empire, its viceroy from Ravenna used the building as part of a guard house to protect the approach to the palace, still on the Palatine. Like the guard house in the imperial palace in Constantinople, it was decorated with Christian murals. As we can tell from archaeological excavation on the site, when the building became the church of S. Maria Antiqua, the original brick piers were replaced by four granite columns surmounted by carved capitals, and an apse was formed out of the solid brick wall mass at the end of the atrium vestibule. From at least the sixth to the ninth centuries, the church was also decorated with marble and mosaic pavements and many wall-paintings, including an early representation of the Virgin Mary as Queen of Heaven, wearing a crown as though belonging to the Imperial court. This splendid structure was not to last long. Partly destroyed in an earthquake in 847, its rights and possessions were transferred to a new church dedicated to Mary, S. Maria Nova within the Temple of Venus and Roma. This explains the epithet – 'Antiqua' for the church discussed here.

In front of S. Maria Antiqua is the Shrine or Oratory of the Forty Martyrs, in origin a hall of the first century AD whose function we do not now know. When it was adapted as a Christian oratory, an apse was added containing frescoes, loosely dated to the sixth to the ninth centuries. These depict forty soldiers who were frozen to death in an icy lake at Sebaste in Armenia in AD 303 during the persecutions of Christians, hence its modern name. It is one of the buildings that has suffered most from modern restoration. In 1999 a large brick structure with a prominent roof of parti-coloured pantiles was built to protect the fragments of the frescoes. A kind of giant Wendy house, improbably provided with its own entry-phone, this absurd structure now dominates many views of the Forum, notably the celebrated view from the gallery of the Tabularium.

### S. MARIA LIBERATRICE

For Piranesi the church of S. Maria Liberatrice was an important landmark in the Forum. It featured prominently in several of his views (figs 1 and 5), defining the south side of the Forum just as the church of S. Lorenzo in Miranda, which it faced across the Via Sacra, defined the north side. In the last of its several forms, this was a handsome Renaissance church of 1617. Originally built in the thirteenth century, it engulfed what remained of the church of S. Maria Antiqua after the earthquake. Its main purpose was to commemorate the nearby site of the home of the legendary dragon, chained by Pope Sylvester I (reigned 314–35) in fulfilment of a command he received from St Peter in a vision. The name 'Liberatrice', referring to the liberation of the inhabitants of Rome from the fearsome dragon, was transferred to the Virgin Mary, to whom the church was dedicated. The site is near the House of the Vestals, who were traditionally supposed to have fed the dragon. In the twelfth-century account known as the *Mirabilia Urbis Romae* (*Marvels of the City of Rome*), we are told that near the Church of St Anthony, or the Oratory of the Forty Martyrs, 'is a place called Hell, because in ancient times it burst forth there and brought great mischief upon Rome'. The author of this curious but gullible work also referred to 'the Temple of Vesta, which – it is said – a dragon crouches beneath, as we read in the life of Saint Silvester'.

The medieval church S. Maria Liberatrice was rebuilt in 1617 with a new façade and cupola from designs by Onorio Longhi (1568–1619), father of the more prolific Martino Longhi the Younger. Onorio was the architect of the vast church of SS. Carlo e Ambrogio al Corso in Rome, begun in 1612. His pedimented entrance front at S. Maria Liberatrice, two-storeyed and adorned with round-headed niches and an order of pilasters, was a miniature version of the late Renaissance façade of 1571–84 by Giacomo della Porta at the influential church of Il Gesù in Rome. Over the crossing at S. Maria Liberatrice, Longhi placed a cupola over a low octagonal drum, a north Italian form. The architect Francesco Ferrari restored and enriched the interior in 1749 with stuccowork and paintings by leading artists of the classicising trend of the day, Sebastiano Ceccarini and Lorenzo Gramiccia, showing the importance then attached to this church.

However, it is now sadly gone. For nearly three centuries,

Longhi's attractive church was a key element of the Forum, but it was doomed when the remains of S. Maria Antiqua, first partially uncovered in 1702, were fully excavated in 1900 by Giacomo Boni. In accordance with the archaeological doctrine that the older anything is the more important it must be, Boni, though supposedly upholding Ruskin's views on sensitive restoration, was bent on demolishing S. Maria Liberatrice in order to expose surviving elements of the original Roman building. In fact, the church proved to have been so solidly built that dynamite was necessary to destroy it. Boni made no proper record of what he had demolished, allowing cartloads of fragments, some featuring faded Early Christian wall-paintings, to be taken away for disposal. During extensive excavations and repairs in 1985–7, the concrete vaults were reconstructed in order to help preserve those paintings that still survive from S. Maria Antiqua, though the church is not normally open to the public.

## S. ADRIANO

An even more striking example of re-use, and restoration, is the church of S. Adriano. Formed in the early seventh century inside the Curia Julia (Senate House) which dates from the late third or early fourth century BC, this church was given a superb Baroque interior in the mid seventeenth century (fig. 25). In its first conversion in AD 630 the marble steps for the senators' seats were retained together with the extravagant decoration and splendid furnishings: indeed, these features were valued so much that the Catholic liturgy had to take place around them. S. Adriano was remodelled in the Romanesque style in the late twelfth or early thirteenth

25. *Senate House, interior as S. Adriano by Martino Longhi the Younger.* The
Senate House, last rebuilt in the late third century AD, was adapted as a
church in the seventh century and subsequently remodelled more than once,
notably in 1653–6 by Longhi whose masterly interior was sadly destroyed in
the 1930s. The pair of Composite columns, suggestive of a triumphal arch,
frame a top-lit space with an elliptical dome, beyond which the coffered
half-dome echoes those in the Temple of Venus and Roma, further east in
the Forum.

century, when a tall campanile was added at the rear and antique columns with richly ornamented bases were introduced as *spolia* into the interior to make a six-bay nave and aisles. These columns were later encased in a Renaissance pier arcade under Pope Sixtus V Peretti (reigned 1585–90), but a more important and complete remodelling was carried out in 1653–6 by Martino Longhi the Younger, whose masterpiece was the dazzling church of SS. Vincenzo ed Anastasio, built for Cardinal Mazarin opposite the Fontana di Trevi. The most daringly inventive of the talented Longhi family of architects, he also published poetry and an architectural treatise.

Longhi reduced the six bays of the existing nave to five, turning the sixth bay into a kind of crossing or transept, crowned by a tall elliptical dome, lit by a cupola. This space was preceded by a pair of giant, free-standing, Composite columns like a triumphal arch and forming a scenographic gesture which was to influence Baroque architects such as Carlo Rainaldi. Longhi replaced the wooden roof with a barrel vault, and over the high altar created a half-dome, its bold diagonal coffering echoing that in the apses of the Temple of Venus and Roma in the Forum. The side chapel of SS. Giorgio e Bacco included succulent details borrowed from Borromini, but Longhi's taste for rich sculptural decoration was nowhere better seen than at S. Adriano in his chapel of the Madonna delle Grazie.

It was not until 1860 that the building which housed Longhi's masterly church was first identified by an archaeologist as the Senate House. From this moment its survival was threatened, though it was not to be deconsecrated until 1935. The Baroque structures were entirely removed between 1935 and

1938, leaving grim, bare walls, which, unlike Longhi's work, give no impression whatever of the richness of the antique Senate House. The present wooden ceiling is also modern. One critic has rightly observed that 'a building such as the Curia offers a warning of the hazards of partial restoration', for it is hard to see the purpose of ripping out the vibrant work of Longhi which imaginatively demonstrated the timeless continuity of the classical language of architecture. In a masterpiece entirely compatible with the ancient structure, Longhi had contrived to combine references to ancient buildings in the Forum, such as the Temple of Venus and Roma, with modern Baroque architecture. Nonetheless, some visitors see what they wish to see, so that another archaeologist claimed that it has now been 'restored to its ancient form'. One even believed that 'it is one of the most splendid interiors to survive from classical Rome.'

## S. LORENZO IN MIRANDA

The one place where it is still possible to appreciate the rich drama of the Baroque Forum is the church of S. Lorenzo in Miranda. For once, a church has happily been suffered to survive within a Roman temple (figs 2 and 5). First recorded in 1074, it was built within the Temple of Antoninus and Faustina, which had been begun in AD 140 by the Emperor Antoninus Pius in honour of his wife. Imitated in antiquity, for example in the 'Temple of Diana' (*c.* AD 200) at Evora, Portugal, it later became familiar through the woodcut illustrations by Palladio in his *Four Books of Architecture* (1570), and by the more sophisticated engravings by Antoine Desgodetz of 1682 in his *Les Edifices antiques de Rome* (*The Ancient*

*Buildings of Rome*). Palladio could not resist 'improving' the temple by setting it in a *temenos* (a walled sacred precinct), probably inspired by that of the Forum of Caesar, and by enriching its interior with statues.

Its fame inspired modern imitations far afield. The external frieze of the temple is carved with scrolls of leaves of the acanthus plant and candelabra placed between pairs of griffins facing each other. Today these are, of course, in a fragmentary and damaged condition so that, except to the specialist, they may be disappointing. Their afterlife, as with so much Roman decorative work, is rather more impressive. For example, this frieze was often imitated in buildings without sacred associations, notably by William Kent in his palatial attempt to create an ancient Roman house at Holkham Hall, Norfolk (1734–65). He based his version on the representation of the frieze by Desgodetz, a fact recorded on a nineteenth-century board handed out to visitors to the house. This cites the same source for details in other interiors which Kent took from the Temple of 'Fortuna Virilis' (Portumnus) and the Basilica of Maxentius in Rome.

In the fifteenth century Pope Eugenius IV not only dismantled the rear wall of the cella to reuse its materials in rebuilding the Lateran Palace but gave the church of S. Lorenzo in Miranda to a guild of apothecaries. Their successors, the Collegio Chimico Farmaceutico, still occupy it, housing their museum in the crypt or lower church. But it is the complete rebuilding of the structure in 1601–14 by Orazio Torriani and the dramatic incorporation of the ancient temple, that give the present church much of its charm. The modern approach to it is disappointing, for visitors to the Forum today, coming from the entrance off the Via dei Fori

Imperiali, first see the bleak and unadorned largely modern office wing at the back of the church. To restore meaning to the building, an entrance should once more be made from its original doorway in the Forum, which should not be difficult to contrive.

Torriani's new façade is crowned by a tall and ebulliently Baroque broken pediment, which was completed later in the seventeenth century. It is a vivid reminder of the appearance of the Forum as the Campo Vaccino (Field of Cows) in the eighteenth century, when it was alive with recent buildings incorporating the remains of ancient Roman ones. The interior of the church with its well-restored paintings is little known or visited, though it contains a high altar by the great Baroque architect and painter Pietro da Cortona (1596–1669).

The staircase up to the portico was excavated in 1876, though the modern one is a displeasing reconstruction of it in inappropriate brick. The row of old houses adjacent to the building on the left was demolished in 1899 to excavate the floor of the Basilica Aemilia. The survival of Torriani's church of S. Lorenzo is astonishing in view of the calls for its destruction by the archaeological purists we have already cited, such as Charlotte Eaton and Horace Marucchi.

### S. FRANCESCA ROMANA

Shown in countless paintings and engravings, more beautiful and infinitely better sited than SS. Cosmas and Damian, the church of S. Francesca Romana, with its Romanesque campanile, is one of the most appealing and dominant buildings in the entire Forum (figs 5 and 26). For nearly 1,200 years it has demarcated the Forum's eastern end. It is thus greatly

26. *S. Francesca Romana exterior (engraving by G. B. Falda, 1665).* This modest engraving hardly does justice to the church with its tall Romanesque campanile and its beautiful façade in gleaming travertine by Carlo Lambardi of 1615. On rising ground near the Arch of Titus, it dominates many views of the Forum. As first built in the ninth century, this church was the first major new building to be built in the Forum since the end of the Empire.

to be regretted that there is no longer any public access to it from the Forum. Instead, visitors have to take a circuitous route up the steep road parallel to the Via dei Fori Imperiali to an area on the side of the church which, though right next to the Basilica of Maxentius, includes an ugly tarmac car park and inhospitable wire fences. With the ecclesiastical rank of a minor basilica like SS. Cosmas and Damian, S. Francesca Romana combines elements of all major periods from antiquity to the Baroque. It is one of the most historic, evocative and appealing buildings in the Forum, where its life and richness make it a unique survival in a setting which archaeologists are doing so much to render unattractive and dispiriting. With a classical entrance façade of 1615 below its twelfth-century campanile featuring tiers of arches decorated with majolica, this church is a focal point on rising ground in the Forum.

Originally founded by Pope Leo IV in 850 as S. Maria Nova, it was the first major new building in the Forum since classical times. Its name was changed to S. Francesca Romana in 1608 to mark the canonization in that year of Francesca Buzzi de' Ponzi (1384–1440), a noblewoman who had founded a Sisterhood of Oblates in the church in 1421. On her husband's death, she entered this herself and was rewarded by God with the visible presence of her guardian angel, with whom she was reported to have conversed familiarly. Regarded as the only native Roman to found a religious order, she was canonised as S. Francesca Romana and her name added to that of the church of S. Maria Nova. In 1926, she became, somewhat improbably, the patron saint of motorists, presumably in recognition of her association with care and guardianship. On her feast day, 9 March, the street

27. With its rich gilt wood ceiling, the broad nave of S. Francesca Romana
is the work of Carlo Lambardi in 1608–15, though the apse at the east end
contains twelfth-century mosaics. Before the apse is a semicircular Baroque
screen of marble columns by Gianlorenzo Bernini, sheltering a later statue of
S. Francesca Romana.

leading up to the church from the Via dei Fori Imperiali is, or was, crowded with cars each year.

The church owes its present form to a remodelling in 1608–15 by Carlo Lambardi, a notable Roman architect, and its façade bears the date 1615. Evidently giving much thought to the design of a new building in this prominent position close to the Arch of Titus, Lambardi chose a temple front with a triumphal-arch theme, incorporating a giant order in travertine. He adopted this form from the similar façades of two Venetian churches of Andrea Palladio, S. Giorgio Maggiore and the Redentore. Though Palladio is probably the most imitated architect in history, especially in Britain and the United States of America, it is most unusual for his work to be echoed at this date in Rome, where his Renaissance style would have seemed out of date.

The interior of S. Francesca Romana in the rich and noble form given it by Lambardi glistens with Baroque gilding and polychromatic marbles (fig. 27). The wide nave, five bays long with a triumphal arch separating it from the apse, has a carved gilt wood ceiling by Lambardi. Behind a grille on the south wall of the south transept is one of the most extraordinary objects in the Forum, which should certainly not be missed by the curious visitor. It is a stone from the Via Sacra with marks that are traditionally the imprints of the knees of St Peter as he prayed for the exposure of the wizardry of Simon Magus, who had challenged him (and possibly St Paul as well), to a competition in levitation in the Forum. By drawing on magical powers, Magus succeeded in flying up to the sky but was killed as he crashed to earth. The site of his fall, brought about by the prayers of St Peter, was in the neighbourhood. The story is a curious echo of the Lacus Curtius, in which a knight is supposed to have sacrificed himself by leaping into a chasm that opened up in the Forum. On another occasion, as recorded in the Acts of the Apostles, Simon Magus tried to bribe St Peter; hence 'simony', the buying or selling of ecclesiastical preferment, is named after him.

At the east end of the church are the substantial buildings of the convent of the Benedictine monks of the Olivetan order, who were given the property in 1352. Largely of medieval origin, remodelled between the sixteenth and eighteenth centuries, the monastic buildings include a beautiful cloister, reconstructed in brick under Alexander VI (reigned 1492–1503), with three storeys of round-headed arcades of different heights. The Renaissance lyric poet and playwright Torquato Tasso and the nineteenth-century Hungarian pianist and composer Franz Liszt, both sought peace in this hidden place. Liszt wrote a symphonic poem about Tasso, whose greatest work was his epic poem *Jerusalem Delivered*, about the First Crusade and the struggles between Christians and Muslims at the end of it.

The south range of the convent, which includes neo-classical work of 1816 by Giuseppe Valadier, shortly before he restored the adjacent Arch of Titus, became state property in 1873, when religious orders were suppressed and the monks dispossessed. It now houses the Soprintendenza Archaeologica di Roma and also the Antiquarium Forense (Museo del Foro), which was established in 1900 by Giacomo Boni for objects largely excavated by himself in the Forum, though with many later additions. Including many fine pieces of sculpture and architectural ornament, the collection is beautifully displayed in a dozen rooms near the cloister, including

28. *S. Giuseppe dei Falegnami, exterior.* The curious and complicated façade of the church of the Carpenters Guild in the north-west corner of the Forum was built in 1599–1602 by the antiquarian G. B. Montano, though work on the church continued until 1663, first by his pupil, G. B. Soria, and finally by A. del Grande. It was built over the ancient Roman Mamertine prison for which the lower portico was constructed as an entrance in 1932.

the rib-vaulted refectory with fifteenth-century frescoes attributed to Antonio da Viterbo.

## S. GIUSEPPE DEI FALEGNAMI

Often overlooked by visitors blinded by archaeology through no fault of their own, is an intriguing group of buildings close together at the west end of the Forum.

Including what can claim to be the most sophisticated building in the entire Forum, the Baroque church of SS. Martina e Luca, these monuments are important for demarcating the north-western extremity of the Forum area. Here, on the north side of the Tabularium, from the present Via di San Pietro in Carcere a Roman road known as the Clivus Argentarius (Bankers' Rise) ran between the Capitol and the Quirinal hills. A surviving section of this road descends to S. Giuseppe dei Falegnami, the church of the Guild of Carpenters, who had been settled here since 1540 (fig. 28). Their church was built over the 'Carcer', the Mamertine Prison, sometimes also known as the Tullianum, either because of the *tullius*, or spring of water, which drained through it, or because it was believed to have been constructed by King Servius Tullius (578–535 BC). It has long been venerated because, according to a legend, St Peter and St Paul were imprisoned here in the reign of Nero, causing the spring to rise miraculously so that they could baptise their fellow prisoners and gaolers. It is a wonderful example of what we have described as the palimpsests, the multiple layers of Christianity and pagan antiquity, which are such a feature of the Forum.

The crypt of S. Giuseppe dei Falegnami, called the Cappella

del Crucifisso after a crucifix discovered in the Forum, was built over two ancient cells, one on top of the other. The upper is trapezoidal in shape, the lower originally circular and earlier in date, possibly of the fourth or third century BC. Formerly reached only by a hole in the roof, this is supposed to have been the death cell where enemies of the State were strangled or died of starvation. These included Jugurtha in 104 BC; fellow conspirators of Catiline, who landed up here thanks to the efforts of Cicero, in 63 BC; and Vercingetorix, who had fought against Caesar, in 52 BC. Sallust, author of an account of Jugurtha, wrote of the condemned cell: 'in the prison there is a place called the Tullianum … about twelve feet deep, closed all round by strong walls and a stone vault. Its aspect is repugnant and fearsome from neglect, darkness and stench.' In the fifteenth century the cell was dedicated as S. Pietro in Carcere.

Building of the Carpenters' Guild church of S. Giuseppe dei Falegnami over this cell was begun in 1599 from designs by the architect and archaeologist Giovanni Battista Montano, a member of the Guild. His inventive reconstructions of ancient Roman buildings, published by his pupil Giovanni Battista Soria, influenced Baroque architects such as Borromini. Montano's entrance façade, completed in 1602, includes volutes, aedicules and two small pediments contained within the larger one. Curiously lacking in carved detail, it looks almost as though it has been refaced in cement. After 1621, Soria continued work on the church, and it was completed in 1663 by Antonio del Grande.

The balustraded double staircase on the façade was mutilated in 1932 to make way for a new and enlarged ground-floor entrance portico in the Mussolini classical style. This was to provide prominent access to what is left of the Mamertine Prison, considered to be of more interest than the church, while at the same time, the adjacent houses on the left were unnecessarily demolished.

## SS. LUCA E MARTINA

A few feet away from S. Giuseppe dei Falegnami is the church of SS. Luca e Martina, a seventeenth-century Baroque masterpiece by Pietro da Cortona, the most distinguished roofed building in or near the Forum (fig. 6). It replaced the Early Christian church of S. Martina, which had been built Pope Honorius I in the early seventh century on the site of the Secretarium Senatus, a special court convened to judge senators, which was built next to the Senate House towards the end of the Empire. Depictions of S. Martina are rare, but its modest, domestic-looking façade with a tiny bell turret can be seen in an engraving of 1575 by Etienne Dupérac.

In 1588 the little church of S. Martina was given to the Accademia di S. Luca, founded in 1577 as an academy of painters, sculptors and architects. Since the evangelist St Luke was traditionally an artist, he became the patron saint of painters. The long influential Accademia di S. Luca, closely allied to the papal court and always a great promoter of interest in antiquity, survives to the present day in the Palazzo Carpegna, near the Fontana di Trevi. It was moved here as one of the many casualties of the creation of Mussolini's great road, the Via dei Fori Imperiali, in 1932, but its important collections survive and are open to the public.

To mark its ownership by the Accademia di S. Luca the name of S. Luca was added to that of S. Martina in 1589, and a wooden model for a new church on a slightly expanded site was made by Giovanni Battista Montano, then lecturing on architecture at the Accademia. No funds were yet available for building, but in 1626 Cardinal Francesco Barberini, nephew of Pope Urban VIII, became protector of the Academy of St Luke, and in 1634 Pietro da Cortona was made its *principe* (head). He was given permission to remodel the crypt or lower church to provide a tomb for himself, but the discovery in it of the body of S. Martina during the excavations in 1634 prompted Cardinal Barberini to pay for an ambitious new church to bring pilgrims to venerate her relics.

Cortona's church of SS. Luca e Martina, built slowly from 1635 to 1673, has a two-storeyed façade with a striking convex form, which was the first of the celebrated curved fronts of the Baroque churches of Rome. The columns of its upper storey are in the Composite order which, as we have noted, is a characteristically rich, even indigestible, Roman invention, its capitals crowning the acanthus leaves of the Corinthian order with the volutes of the Ionic order. Cortona doubtless chose this order because of the proximity of the Arch of Septimius Severus, which is also Composite. Piranesi must have seen this parallel when he included the arch and the church together in his *Vedute di Roma*. In his day, when the arch was almost half-buried, its sumptuous capitals would have been much nearer to eye-level. Architects working in the Forum found various ways of relating their buildings to earlier ones, and the dialogue Cortona conducts between his church and the adjacent arch is one of the most brilliant. He was also careful to place the cornice surmounting his ground floor at the same level as the crowning cornice of the more modest but adjacent Curia.

29. *SS. Luca e Martina, nave.* Work on this dynamic Baroque masterpiece by
Pietro da Cortona began in 1635 and continued on the interior for over forty
years, after his death in 1669. The absence of the colour often associated with
Baroque interiors heightens the impact of the powerful architectural forms,
especially the massed Ionic columns and piers, which are thus allowed to
dominate the space.

The domed cruciform interior of SS. Luca e Martina has none of the colour we associate with the Baroque, but it is an emphatically architectural essay in plastic form, dominated by massive unfluted columns in greyish-white travertine (fig. 29). This is in astonishing contrast to the richly coloured crypt, which is not normally open but should not be missed (fig. 30). Joseph Connors described romantically in 1982 how, while the upper church 'is executed in white travertine and stucco, rich effects of colour are displayed in the crypt … [where the] complex system of staircases, dark corridors, and small Hadrianic chambers is meant to evoke the feeling of mystery experienced by seventeenth-century explorers of the crypts and catacombs of early Christian Rome.' Indeed, in the centre of the shallow apse of the inner chapel in the crypt is an Early Christian throne, preserved from the original church.

The walls are lined with different marbles in a rich variety of colours and pattern, re-creating the appearance of the buildings of Augustan Rome in and around the Forum. There are fine statues and reliefs by sculptors including Alessandro Algardi and Cosimo Fancelli, while in the inner chamber, Cortona's centrally placed altar containing the relics of S. Martina is in elaborately carved gilt bronze, now darkened but originally showing a dazzling sparkle.

With its prominent dome and powerful interiors, SS. Luca e Martina is one of the most impressive Baroque churches in Rome, but its impact has been impaired by the processes of archaeology, which have insulated it from the urban setting for which it was designed: first by the lowering of the level of the Forum after 1802, and then by the destruction of the adjacent buildings in 1932 to expose the foundations of ancient remains. The removal of the houses that flanked the church

30. *SS. Luca e Martina, crypt.* Pietro da Cortona's sumptuously polychromatic crypt is in marked contrast to the austere church above, thus stressing the importance of the relics of S. Martina in the gilt bronze altar seen in this view. The walls are lined with richly coloured and varied marbles creating the most powerful impression anywhere in the Forum of the splendour of Roman imperial interiors.

emphasised the fact that Cortona had been unable to complete the façade. As Anthony Blunt complained in 1982, 'As it stands now the church is in many ways awkward and naked.'

We have stressed in this chapter the gripping way in which the religions of the classical and the Christian world interlock culturally and architecturally at every level in this extraordinarily iconic place, the Roman Forum. Since the visitor who misses this challenge of the relationship of ancient and modern will miss much of what the Forum has to offer, it is hoped that this book will help to rescue the Forum from its ugly and depressing role as an 'archaeological site', and to reinstate it as an evocative place of haunting and resonant beauty. This might confirm the claim of T. S. Eliot who, considering the 'conformity between the old and the new' in his famous essay, 'Tradition and the Individual Talent', observed that we 'will not find it preposterous that the past should be altered by the present as much as the present is directed by the past'.

# FROM THE RENAISSANCE TO
# THE GRAND TOUR

## THE RISE OF ARCHAEOLOGY AND THE
## DESTRUCTION OF THE MONUMENTS

Between late antiquity and the Middle Ages, when Rome shrunk dramatically in size, the monuments in the Forum were largely abandoned and little visited. The celebrated Temple of Castor and Pollux was already in a ruinous state by the fourth century, while all that survived of it in the fifteenth century were the three columns we see today. Hadrian's fabulous Temple of Venus and Roma fell into decay after its bronze roof tiles were taken away in the seventh century for re-use at St Peter's, while even the Arch of Titus was engulfed by fortifications in the twelfth century. However, other temples and basilicas still survived more or less intact until, ironically, the Renaissance. By the early sixteenth century, when the population of Rome had risen to 55,000, the Forum had been invaded by cottages and houses with gardens, as can be seen in a drawing by Heemskerck of *c.* 1534. It remained in much the same state for three or four hundred years.

We have seen how some of the monuments in the Forum were adapted as churches, with S. Francesca Romana, established in the ninth century, as the only large wholly new church. We can gain an impression of the Forum between the twelfth century and the early Renaissance from what was the standard guidebook to Rome until the fifteenth century, *Mirabilia Urbis Romae* (*Marvels of the City of Rome*). It was probably written by a twelfth-century canon of St Peter's, who divided his perambulation of Rome into sixteen sections, reaching the Forum in the tenth section. That he chose to deal with it in less than a single page suggests its relative lack of importance at this time.

However, from the fourteenth century, students of antiquity such as Petrarch (1304–74), the restorer of classical scholarship, complained of the growing deterioration of the monuments. Those responsible for causing this damage included Pope Urban V (1362–70), who granted materials from the Temple of Antoninus and Faustina in the Forum for use in building the Lateran Palace in 1364. This was on condition that the chapel of S. Lorenzo in Miranda, which had been set up in the portico of the temple, remained undisturbed. Despite the passion for Greek and Latin classics of Pope Nicholas V (reigned 1447–55), he removed ancient stones from the Forum and the Colosseum.

Up till about 1500, papal permission was occasionally given to builders to pull down ancient edifices for the provision of building stone, or even to those who wished to burn marble statues or marble blocks in kilns in order to produce lime. In all cases, one third of the profit had to be handed over to the Camera Apostolica (Apostolic Chamber). In the Forum, the Temple of Venus and Roma went in this way in 1450, as did the House of the Vestals in 1499. In a vain attempt to halt this process, Pope Pius II, an architectural patron and neo-antique enthusiast, promoted a bull in 1462 which ordered the conservation of the ancient monuments of Rome on historic, aesthetic and also moral grounds, since they were seen as reminding us of the evanescence of earthly fortunes.

It was, ironically, when these monuments were treated as quarries for building stone from the fifteenth century, leading to the lime kilns, that guidebooks to the buildings which survived began to appear. An important early example, by Poggio Bracciolini, papal bureaucrat, scholar and discoverer of manuscripts of lost Latin texts, was 'Descriptio urbis Romae et de ruina eiusdem' ('Description of the City of Rome and its Ruins"), the first book of his *De Varietate Fortunae* (*On the Variety of Fortune*) of 1448. Noting the dilapidated state of the monuments, he regretted that so little of the Temple of Saturn had survived the lime-kilns. Though it was not a systematic account, he analysed different layers and also different materials as evidence for dating, notably in the Forum at the vestibule to SS. Cosmas and Damian, noting walling of *opus quadratum*, that is, squared ashlar laid in regular courses. Like many subsequent visitors, Poggio also wandered among the ruins, writing how he was 'in imagination carrying myself back to the times when senatorial speeches were delivered here, and pretending that I am listening to Lucius Crassus, Hortensius or Cicero orating'.

The writings of Poggio Bracciolini can be seen as part of an outburst of activity in the early fifteenth century after the return of the popes from Avignon to Rome late in the previous century. The hope that the papacy might now take over the function of the Roman Empire and re-create the Pax Romana was expressed by Flavio Biondo, humanist and papal secretary, in his *Roma Instaurata* (*Rome Restored*) of *c.* 1445, dedicated to Eugenius IV. In the first reconstruction of the ancient city, Biondo aimed to replace with objective truth the fantasies and errors of the twelfth-century *Mirabilia Urbis Romae*. He lamented the continuing destruction of ancient Rome but claimed to have found traces of the Temple of Janus in the Forum. In another book, *Roma Triumphans*, he tried to locate the Comitium in the Forum, but regretted that the few traces of foundations were still being burnt for lime. In a more hopeful mood came Andrea Fulvio, whose poem *Antiquaria Urbis* (1514) stressed the connection between ancient and modern, that is papal, Rome. Associated with Raphael in studying the antiquities of Rome, he published a guidebook to the city, *Antiquitates Urbis* (1527).

Archaeology, which has had for centuries so profound an impact on the appearance of the Forum, and still does today, was an invention of the Renaissance. It was then a tool for uncovering the past to provide a model for the present and the future. The attempt to re-establish antiquity as the basis of modern life led authors such as Leon Battista Alberti and Fra Giovanni Giocondo to study the *Ten Books of Architecture* by Vitruvius, the only architectural treatise to survive from antiquity. This work inspired Alberti's *De Re Aedificatoria* (*On the Art of Building*), the manuscript of which he presented to Pope Nicholas V in *c.* 1452, while Fra Giocondo published an illustrated edition of Vitruvius in 1511. Vitruvius had said virtually nothing on the Roman Forum which, when he was writing, cannot have looked very impressive, as the additions to it of Julius Caesar were only just beginning. The crowded and irregular Roman Forum was not part of the orderly and rational world of classicism that Vitruvius wished to re-create. His account of forums in general was inspired by the very different regular colonnaded forums of the Greeks. Nor did

Sebastian Serlio, writing in the sixteenth century, mention the Roman Forum in his rich and monumental *L'Architettura*, published in instalments from 1537 to 1575.

Following the lead given by architects and writers such as Alberti, Fra Giocondo, Donato Bramante and Serlio, ancient Roman buildings had come to be more valued by the early sixteenth century than at any time since antiquity. Yet it is one of the great paradoxes of European cultural history that, despite this, the process of destruction in the Forum continued. This was in order to recycle the materials for new monuments that, it was not doubted, would rival those of antiquity. Bramante is supposed to have taken travertine blocks from the Basilica Julia for his own buildings, while the temples of Saturn, Vespasian and Vesta were similarly dismantled. Even the Temple of Janus, discovered in 1531, was soon destroyed by Cardinal Jean du Bellay, who was, ironically, a humanist, archaeologist and collector of antique sculpture. However, Giuliano da San Gallo, who shared the responsibility for St Peter's with Raphael and Fra Giocondo from 1513, made many drawings of ancient Roman buildings, including one showing the rich ornamentation of the now-destroyed Basilica Aemilia in the Forum, which had long been used as a stone quarry (fig. 19). In his Villa Medici at Poggio a Caiano near Florence (*c.* 1480–*c.* 1497), San Gallo used his knowledge of antiquity to design perhaps the first neo-antique house with a pedimented portico.

Fra Giocondo had already complained of the destruction of ancient stones, but Pope Leo X during his reign from 1513 to 1522 encouraged research by antiquarians in Rome, and in 1515 he appointed Raphael to oversee the preservation of marbles, especially those bearing ancient inscriptions, imposing heavy fines for infractions. Raphael was also to determine whether other Roman remains should be preserved or used for the construction of St Peter's, of which he had been appointed Architect in Chief in 1514. Leo X, who worshipped Raphael and his paintings and hoped to make him a cardinal, was the pope into whose mouth were put the glorious words, 'God has given us the papacy. Let us enjoy it!' The principal architect employed in Florence by his father, Lorenzo the Magnificent, was Giuliano da San Gallo, who now, in the newly sympathetic artistic climate established by the pope, presented him with his drawings of ancient Roman monuments.

The Sack of Rome in 1527 by the armies of Emperor Charles V, long-unpaid ruffians who were now anxious for loot, did no significant damage to the ancient monuments. However, Pope Paul III (reigned 1534–49) appointed his private secretary, Latino Manetti, to oversee the Forum and 'preserve all statues, inscriptions and blocks of marble, free them from brushwood and ivy, and prevent the erection of new buildings on them, or their destruction, conversion into lime or removal from the city.' Since the ancient roads in the Forum had become blocked by debris and earth, Paul III created a new one in 1534 passing through the Arch of Septimius Severus on its way to Castel Sant' Angelo. This was in preparation for the triumphal entry of Charles V two years later, following his retaking of Tunis from Barbarossa and the Turks. The new road caused some destruction in the Forum, for it involved the demolition of 200 houses and four churches, though Pope Paul also created temporary triumphal arches modelled on the Arch of Constantine. His opening up of the Forum, which created a wide, empty space in the centre, also enabled it to flourish once more as a market, an agreeable place in which to stroll and a centre for artists, although this did not prevent further destruction of the monuments.

The procession of Charles V was the model for the triumphal processions of monarchs and generals that took place in Europe until the end of the eighteenth century. It was also a parallel to those undertaken by newly elected popes, who passed through the Forum on their way from the Vatican to their coronation, which normally took place until 1870 in the cathedral of Rome, St John Lateran. The election of forty-one popes between 1503 and 1846 meant that the Forum was frequently a lively focus of ritual. The *Cavalcata*, as the procession was known, consisted of hundreds of people accompanied by trumpeters, lackeys leading mules laden with treasures, twenty-four pages, and the Swiss Guard, after whom the pope rode on a white palfrey. It was recorded of the *Cavalcata* of Clement XIV in 1769 that, 'Perhaps the greatest crowd to see the procession was in and about the Forum, where the comparatively open space afforded a better chance of viewing all its magnificence. Every inch of ground was occupied, even the spaces between the columns of the temples of Antoninus and Castor and Pollux.' This was the last *Cavalcata* at which the pope rode on a horse. In 1776, Pius VI chose to be conveyed in a magnificent state coach drawn by six horses, described as 'very much after the fashion of a Roman triumph'.

On 22 July 1540, Pope Paul III handed over exclusive permission for the excavation of antiquities to the Deputies of the Fabric of St Peter's, a clear indication to them that anything could go. The period of greatest destruction was from 1540 to 1550, when the marble steps in front of the Temple of Antoninus and Faustina, and, as we noted in Chapter 3, the

Temple of Divus Julius, were reduced to lime, in the cause of St Peter's. The whole roadway from the Arch of Titus to the Temple of Antoninus and Faustina became a quarry. Clearly visible below the capitals of the columns of this temple are deep incisions that may have been made about this time to secure ropes in the vain hope of pulling the columns down. A simpler explanation is that they were for the attachment of banners at festivals; indeed, they are shown in a drawing attributed to Marten van Heemskerck when the Forum was being prepared for the triumphal entry of the Emperor Charles V in 1536.

The destruction of the monuments was watched with distress by the architect, archaeologist, and artist Pirro Ligorio, who complained that 'ruins were sold like oxen for the meat-market'. He reported being present at the impressive discovery in the Forum on 15 August 1546 of the famous consular *fasti*, the stone tablets which comprise two main lists: one of consuls from the early fifth century down to Augustus, the other of *triumphators* (generals who had celebrated a triumph) from Romulus himself down to the same period. These were regarded as of enormous importance, almost as the key to Roman history, encouraging a new generation of writers on that subject. Venerated like the tablets of Moses, they were removed in 1548 to Michelangelo's Palazzo dei Conservatori on the Capitoline Hill where, as the *fasti Capitolini*, they can still be seen. The design of their frame has, almost inevitably, been attributed to Michelangelo, in view of the high regard in which he has always been held.

Ligorio was shocked that the monument in the Forum where the *fasti* had been found, which he believed to be the Arch of Augustus, had been ruthlessly torn down and

[ 143 ]

destroyed in thirty days during the excavations. Its materials were to be refashioned or ground up for the building of St Peter's. He made a beautiful but fanciful restoration drawing of the arch in quadrifons form, that is, with an opening on each of its four fronts. This was part of his encyclopedia of antiquities for which he left many drawings. His claim that some of the *fasti* had been found attached to a quadrifons arch was discredited in the nineteenth century, when most believed that they had been on the Regia, the ritual centre of Rome. Archaeological opinion has now once more swung to the belief that they were on an arch, but not a four-way one.

Like Alberti, Pirro Ligorio believed that classical antiquity, particularly Roman, should be the model for the contemporary world. He restored the Pantheon and excavated Hadrian's Villa at Tivoli, primarily to discover sculpture; but he also wrote a learned monograph on the villa, which was published posthumously. A sophisticated and learned architect, his work included the Villa d'Este and its gardens at Tivoli, as well as the elegant Casino for Pius IV in the Vatican Gardens. While in papal employ as Architect of the Vatican Palace, he produced his great 'Imago', or topographical reconstruction, of ancient Rome. With twelve engraved sheets totalling about four by five feet, this map had a vertical projection and depicted houses and streets. Remarkably, Pirro Ligorio produced this before the discovery in 1562 at SS. Cosma and Damian in the Forum of fragments of the Marble Plan of Rome that we described in Chapter 2.

In the meantime, the drawing made by Giuliano da San Gallo of the rich surviving portion of the west side of the Basilica Aemilia shortly before its demolition in *c.* 1500 (fig. 19) was echoed in his church of S. Biagio (1518–34) at

Montepulciano in Tuscany. From this antique source come details such as its walls supporting tunnel vaults, as well as its engaged Doric columns and pilasters with, unusually, rosettes in their necking bands. The largest and most important church project of its date in Italy after St Peter's, S. Biagio gives us some idea of what Bramante's St Peter's would have been like. It is therefore ironical that the Basilica Aemilia should have been demolished by Bramante, who is supposed to have re-used its marble blocks in the Palazzo Giraud-Torlonia. Nonetheless, Antonio Labacco pointed out in his *Libro* (1552), in which he published a reconstruction of the basilica, that its 'capricious character' with 'mixed orders' including square Doric piers 'fluted in the Composite style', had appealed to Bramante.

The inventive approach of Renaissance architects to antiquity is also shown in the fictive attic storey with an inscription in a panel that Giuliano da San Gallo added to the Basilica Aemilia in his drawing of it. This reminds us that in a place as ancient as the Forum, in which most monuments have been largely destroyed, there are very few sources on which we can safely rely. It is possible that Antonio da San Gallo the Younger (1484–1546), nephew of Giuliano, drew on the 'Temple of Romulus' in the Forum, with its concave façade and emerging rotunda, for the design of his Mint in Rome of 1526–34.

With the rise of archaeology as a discipline in the sixteenth century, guidebooks began to appear as well as great volumes of engravings, such as Antonio Lafreri's *Speculum Romanae Magnificentiae* (1528–1606), Giovanni Bartolomeo Marliani's *Antiquae Romae Topographia* (1544) and Etienne Dupérac's *Urbis Romae Sciographia* (1574). Palladio, who probably met

Ligorio while he was making his own measured drawings at Hadrian's Villa, published two pocket-sized guidebooks to Rome in 1554, *The Antiquities of Rome* and *Description of the Churches, Stations of the Cross, Indulgences, and Relics of the Bodies of Saints, in the City of Rome*, a book which shows this Renaissance classical architect set in a deeply Catholic mould, citing, for example, S. Maria Liberatrice as the home of the terrible dragon whose mouth was bound by St Sylvester.

Of the still unexcavated Forum, Palladio could say little more than that it began 'at the Arch of Septimius Severus, and went as far as the church of SS. Cosmas and Damian. Its ornamentation was exceedingly beautiful.' However, much later in life, he published an important early record of buildings in the Forum in his influential *I Quattro Libri dell'Architettura* (*Four Books of Architecture*) of 1570. This guide for practising architects and their patrons, in which he described and illustrated his own buildings as well as ancient Roman ones, helped him became the most imitated architect in history. However, even had he wanted to, he was unable to give any impression of the Forum as a whole, because it had not yet been excavated, though perhaps he did not illustrate or describe the half-buried Arch of Septimius Severus or the Arch of Titus, encumbered by later buildings, because he felt they were unlikely to be of much practical use to a modern architect. He did, though, model his temporary triumphal arch for the reception of Henri III in Venice in 1574 on the Arch of Constantine.

Of the buildings in the Forum, Palladio chose to represent four temples (fig. 11) and the Basilica of Maxentius, though he was forced to rely on his imagination for their plans, since their footings were still buried. However, his beautiful and accurate drawings of their columns, capitals and entablatures have been used by countless architects up to the present day, as is testified by the much-used copy of his book in the office of the present-day classical architect, Quinlan Terry.

The ignorance of the Forum that prevailed when Palladio first visited it in the 1540s with his patron, Count Giangiorgio Trissino, is still clear from passages such as this in his *Four Books*:

> *Near the Forum Romanum between the Campidoglio and the Palatine one can see three Corinthian columns which, according to some, were on the side of the Temple of Vulcan, and according to others, of the Temple of Romulus; still others say they belonged to the Temple of Jupiter Stator.*

Palladio plumped for the last of these, though it is in fact the Temple of Castor and Pollux. As it was damaged and partly concealed by earth, Palladio wrongly showed it with fifteen not eleven side columns, and rising up from a high base, not a stepped basement. Similarly, he identified the Temple of Saturn as that of Concord, and gave it eleven side columns, not the thirteen it originally had. The plan he provided of the Temple of Vespasian, which he called Jupiter the Thunderer, bore little relation to reality, since the temple was buried in soil, almost up to the capitals of its three surviving columns.

Having seen in the present book that we still do not know the function of a number of the buildings in the Forum, it may be reassuring to find that there were many more in this category in Palladio's day. However, he well demonstrated how the ruins served to inspire attempts to give shape to what only partially existed. His claim that 'The Forum offers the pilgrim not the spectacle of ancient glory but rather the possibility of re-creating it,' led, as we have seen, to his provision of the temple of Antoninus and Faustina with a handsome walled precinct. His reference to 'The temple once dedicated to Peace, of which the remains can be seen near the church of S. Maria Nova on the Via Sacra', was, of course, to the Basilica of Maxentius, then identified as the Temple of Peace. In reconstructing its façade in a woodcut, Palladio gave it a double pediment, which he echoed in the elevations of the churches he designed in Venice. The identification until 1819 of the Basilica of Maxentius as the prestigious Temple of Peace made it one of the Roman buildings most frequently studied and drawn by Renaissance architects, from Alberti and Serlio onwards. Their engravings of it, as well as Palladio's woodcuts, were to influence church design till at least the time of Christopher Wren in the seventeenth century.

## RENAISSANCE TRAVELLERS

With the arrival in Rome in 1580 of the French author and sceptical essayist Michel de Montaigne, we find a growing feeling for the suggestive power of the monuments as ruins. His responses to Rome are thought to have been coloured by his shock at the effects of the Wars of Religion in France, for he fled to Rome to escape the violence of civil strife. However, a recent scholar has claimed that, 'In Rome there were sights no less moving, the ruins of places wherein his heroes had lived.' In Montaigne's record of his visit there from November 1580 to April 1581, not written for publication, we certainly find little of his usual scepticism. All he could say after visting the Forum was that, 'in many cases we were walking on the top of entire houses. It is easy to judge by the Arch of Severus, that we are more than two pikes' length above the ancient street level; and in truth, almost everywhere you walk on the top of old walls which the rain and the coach ruts uncover.'

Turning to England, we find a country whose cultural as well as religious links with Rome had been severed by the Reformation. The classics were, of course, known, while in 1601 an English translation by Philemon Holland was published of Pliny's *Natural History*, containing, as we saw in Chapter 3, his enthusiastic account of buildings in Rome and the Forum. Rome also lived powerfully in the imagination of William Shakespeare, who included the city in as many as five plays and in one narrative poem. In *Julius Caesar* (*c.* 1599), which he based on a recent English version of Plutarch's *Lives*, Shakespeare memorably re-creates Mark Antony's speech in the Forum to the mob, who impulsively burn Caesar's corpse near the Temple of Castor and Pollux.

By contrast, anti-Catholic, or anti-Italian, prejudice still informed Thomas Nashe, the brilliant wit, pamphleteer and playwright who visited Rome in 1587 and described Italy in a picaresque novel as a place where foreigners 'learn the art of atheism, the art of epicurising, the art of whoring, the art of poisoning, the art of sodomitry'. Similar moral criticisms were made by Francis Osborne, who warned in *Advice to a Son* (1656) that, 'Who travels in Italy, handsome, young, and beardless', will have to protect himself as much 'from the lust of men as the charms of women'.

A very different approach was adopted by Shakespeare's near contemporary the brilliant masque designer and architect Inigo Jones (1573–1652), the first Renaissance architect in Britain. He visited Rome on his cultural travels around Italy in 1613–14 with the young Earl of Arundel, a diplomat and important collector of antiquities. The two of them may be said to have established the popularity of the Grand Tour with the English, for whom it was to play an increasingly important role during the eighteenth century. The host for Jones and Arundel's stay in Rome for five months in 1614 was the discerning patron Marchese Vincenzo Giustiniani. He, rather improbably, arranged for Arundel to excavate in the Forum so as to unearth statues which he had carefully planted there for him. Jones, who was presumably present at this farce, had already included buildings inspired by the Forum in his scene 'The Fallen House of Chivalry' in the court masque *Prince Henry's Barriers*, in 1610.

The church of S. Lorenzo in Miranda, completed in 1614 behind the portico of the Temple of Antoninus and Faustina in the Forum (figs 2 and 5), may have been in Jones's mind when he added a neo-antique portico to the west front of the medieval Old St Paul's Cathedral from 1633. Jones's immense unpedimented portico, the largest north of the Alps, was also inspired by the Temple of Venus and Roma, on the edge of the Forum, as restored by Palladio in *The Four Books of Architecture* (fig. 11). In his copy of this book, Jones made copious notes on this temple, referred to by Palladio as the Temple of the Sun and Moon.

Early Grand Tourists could also make use of a book published in 1654 under the title *The Court of Rome, Wherein is sett forth the whole government thereof ... And a Direction for such as shall Travell to Rome*. The first part was translated from Italian by Henry Cogan, a friend of Inigo Jones, who dedicated it to Sir Justinian Isham. After the death of Jones, Isham employed his former pupil John Webb to rebuild his house, Lamport Hall, Northamptonshire, in a Jonesian Palladian manner in 1655–7. The second part of Cogan's book, also translated from Italian, was a guidebook to Rome that was divided, rather like a modern one, into ten tours of a day each. The Forum was reached on the sixth day's tour, which was called 'From Saint Salvatore del Lauro by Campo Vaccino, and by le Carine'. Tastes have changed so much that the sites which began and ended this day's tour are scarcely, if at all, mentioned in modern guides: S. Salvatore in Lauro is a modest Renaissance church of 1594, since much altered, near the Tiber north of the Chiesa Nuova; while the Carinae, mentioned by Flavio Biondo, was a fashionable residential quarter of ancient Rome on the slopes of the Esquiline behind the Forum.

In the guide translated by Cogan, the reasonably accurate account of the Forum is nearly two and half pages long. Towards the end of it, we reach the 'Temple of Peace' (Basilica of Maxentius) where

*Hereunto adjoyning is the Church of Santa Maria Nuova, wherein lies the Body of St Francesa Romana: in the Garden of this Monasterie are the ruines of two antient edifices to be seen, which some think were two Temples erected to the Sunn, and Moon; others to Concord and Esculapius; and others to Isis and Serapis.*

At this point the text has become a charming medley of saints, monks, gardens and historical confusion.

31. *Farnese Gardens (engraving by G. B. Falda, c. 1670).* Formed in 1610–35 for Cardinal Odoardo Farnese, this terraced section of the extensive Orti Farnesiani largely survives today. Overlooking the Forum from the northern slope of the Palatine, it is aligned on to the central arch of the Basilica of Maxentius opposite. The twin pavilions were originally aviaries surmounted by open-work metal domes which have since been replaced by pyramidal tiled roofs.

A new appreciation of the aesthetic potential of the Forum is reached in the late sixteenth century in the pavilions, grotto and related terraces of the Orti Farnesiani (Farnese Gardens), laid out on the north side of the Palatine to command views across the Forum. These were created for Pope Paul III's grandson, Cardinal Alessandro Farnese, who acquired the property piecemeal with his two brothers from 1542 to 1565. He carried out the first phase in 1570–89, possibly from designs by the major papal architect Giacomo Barozzi da Vignola. In giving a classical cast to Renaissance gardens by associating them with the physical remains of antiquity, Cardinal Farnese was following the now largely forgotten example of Monsignor Euralio Silvestri, who had created an enchanting garden behind the Basilica of Maxentius. He was even allowed by Paul III in 1547 to extend his gardens on to the top of the ruined basilica, then of course lower than today because still in part buried. Here he created hanging terraced gardens which survived until the basilica was excavated in 1828, while parts of the lower gardens were not destroyed until the creation of the Via dei Fori Imperiali in 1932.

The far more architectural gardens which Cardinal Farnese created opposite those of Silvestri were laid out in three long terraces connected by ramps and stairs. They were separated from the Forum by a long and massive wall with a monumental two-storeyed entrance gateway in the centre, designed by Girolamo del Duca, sculptor, architect, garden designer and assistant to Michelangelo. The rusticated ground floor of this gateway is flanked by powerful Doric columns, while the first floor takes the form of a tall arched opening with a balcony serving as a belvedere. This building may be related to the temporary festival arches that were erected in the Forum for the ceremonial procession known as the *possesso* (possession) which marked the accession of a pope.

The long wall with its gateway was demolished in 1880–81 to facilitate excavation of the fragmentary remains of the House of the Vestals which lay below it. However, the beautiful gateway was re-erected in 1958 as the main entrance to the Palatine from the east in the Via di San Gregorio. Apart from this entrance portal, what survives of the Orti Farnesiani today dates from the second phase, carried out by Cardinal Odoardo Farnese in 1610–35 (fig. 31). This is the central entrance ramp and stairs leading uphill from near the House of Vestals to the Cryptoporticus, a stone-faced nymphaeum with a façade in the form of a Palladian arch. Decorated with now-decayed frescoes and oval niches, this contains a large frostwork grotto sheltering a fountain. A groin-vaulted, lateral passage way has stairs at either end which lead up eventually to a pair of two-storeyed casinos with arched openings on the first floor below pantiled roofs of shallow pyramidal form. These roofs replace low domes of ogee profile made of open-work metal, for these two buildings were originally aviaries. They were designed by Girolamo Rainaldi, chief papal architect to Innocent X from 1644, and father of the more brilliant Carlo Rainaldi. He did not place them at right angles to each other but, unexpectedly, at a canted angle. Between the pavilions, sadly closed off at the time of writing, is an ambitious fountain.

This classically inspired paradise is one of the most beautiful and evocative parts of the Forum to which it was a creative response. Ingeniously conceived as a theatre to command views of the Forum, its central axis, from the gateway up to the Cryptoporticus, was aligned directly on the central vault of the Basilica of Maxentius. This produces a dramatic effect that can still be enjoyed today. In his novel *Rome* (1896), Émile Zola wrote of the huge arches of the Basilica of Maxentius that, viewed from the Farnese Gardens, 'they look like porches built for a nation of giants'. He also reacted with considerable perception to the Forum itself as 'a long, clean, livid trench' in which 'piles of foundations appear like bits of bone', so that 'this searched and scoured spot is a city's cemetery … whence rises the intense sadness that envelops dead nations'.

Until 1861, the gardens remained the property of the Farnese family, later represented by the Bourbon family in Naples, though the gardens were already falling into decay. The poet Samuel Rogers recorded in 1814 that, like the ancient ruins, 'The Orti Farnese have now themselves given way. The terraces are dismantled – the aviaries a ruin.' They were sold in 1861 for £10,000 to the Emperor Napoleon III, who had intervened militarily on behalf of Pius IX during the Roman Republic in 1849, thus reversing the treatment of Pius VI by his uncle, Napoleon I. His interest was not in the Farnese Gardens but in what lay under them. Thus, in 1861 the architect Pietro Rosa began to conduct excavations that were continued by the Italian government after the Emperor sold the gardens to the city of Rome in 1870. The next year he left for exile and death at Chislehust in Kent, a sad and rather suburban end for someone accustomed to living in the palaces of St Cloud, the Tuileries and Fontainebleau. We have already noted that Lanciani hated the gardens so much in 1882 that he saw them as the product of original sin. Further excavations were carried out in 1911–25 by Giacomo Boni who, though exposing much of the rubble, also carried out a sympathetic replanting. Indeed, he chose to be buried here under a palm-tree in 1925.

The only large-scale topographically exact view of Rome painted by Claude Lorraine (1600–1682), who arrived in the city in 1627, depicts the Forum on the eve of major changes. His painting shows a muddy space as a setting for low life, containing cattle and a bull chased by dogs, almost the wasteland it had been in the Middle Ages. Its south side is bounded by the high retaining walls of the Farnese Gardens, its north side by a few mean houses, and its east side by the long convent buildings of S. Francesca Romana, which incorporated the Arch of Titus. This central area served as a sheep and cattle pasture, used twice a week since the late sixteenth century for a noisy and smelly cattle market.

However, shortly after this painting was made, the crumbling Early Christian and medieval churches in and surrounding the Forum were lavishly rebuilt. The rustic character of the open ground in the Forum now seemed unacceptable. Thus Fabio Chigi, Pope Alexander VII (reigned 1655–67), made a plan for beautifying Rome with streets and processional ways lined with elm trees or mulberry trees, including a double avenue of elms in the Forum. Running from the Arch of Titus to the Arch of Septimius Severus, this was planted in 1656 (fig. 32).

The pope created this suburban public green to help raise the tone of the Forum, banning the cattle market for the same reason, though it returned in 1659. Another aim of the avenue was to improve access for visitors to the numerous recently

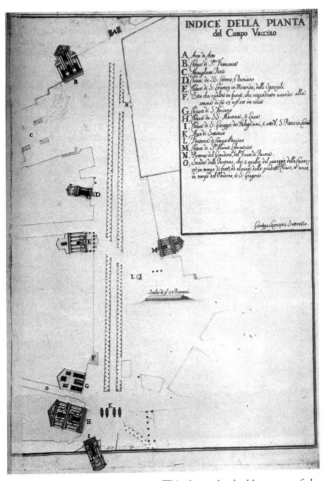

**INDICE DELLA PIANTA**
del Campo Vaccino

A. *Arco di Tito*
B. *Chiesa di S. Francesca*
C. *Templum Pacis*
D. *Chiesa de SS. Cosmo, e Damiano*
E. *Chiesa di S. Lorenzo in Miranda, delli Spezzali*
F. *Sito che è altro in piano, che riquadrato ascende alla somma di 9 et 10 et in circa*
G. *Chiesa di S. Adriano*
H. *Chiesa de SS. Martina, e Luca*
I. *Chiesa di S. Giuseppe dei Falegnami, e sott.° S. Pietro in carcere*
K. *Arco di Settimio*
L. *Fontana di Campo Vaccino*
M. *Chiesa di S. Maria Liberatrice*
N. *Portone del Giardino, del Vasai di Parma*
O. *Strada delle Paraura, che è quella del passaggio delle carroz... in tempo di festa dà alcuni delle predette chiese, et anco in tempo del Verdure, è S. Gregorio*

*Giorgio Lonnini Scritto*

*Scala di p.i 150 Romani*

32. *Plan of the Forum, drawn in c. 1656.* This shows the double avenue of elms which was planted in 1656 by Pope Alexander VII. Leading from the Arch of Titus to the Arch of Septimius Severus, it formed part of his project of beautifying the Forum and of improving access to the churches. Hence their inclusion in this plan.

improved churches around the Forum on festive days. This is clear from the plan made for the pope of the project, which includes drawings of the façades of the churches, identified on a key, but with no reference to the ancient Roman monuments. Pope Alexander VII was an antiquarian and a major architectural patron who realised his vision of Rome as an imperial capital through his extensive patronage of the leading Baroque architects, Bernini, Borromini, Rainaldi and Pietro da Cortona. Indeed, in form and function the avenue in the Forum has been compared to the celebrated colonnade which Bernini erected in the Piazza San Pietro for the same pope. His avenue in the Forum consisted of double rows of elms, the central avenue for carriages or sedan chairs and the side alleys for pedestrians. Its last remains were swept away in the 1880s, but it ought to be re-created today, for its welcome shade would make visiting the Forum a more pleasant experience.

The pull of Rome and its ruins found a creative expression in Claude Lorraine, whose work we have already noted. During his lengthy stay of fifty-five years until his death in 1682, his particular genius was to take the temples of Saturn, Antoninus and Faustina, and Castor and Pollux, in the Forum, and echo them in the romantic columned ruins in the background of his evocative landscape paintings. These temples were, of course, more attractive models for this purpose at that time, when none of their substructures or foundations had been excavated and left exposed as today. Claude's paintings of Arcadian landscapes with their Picturesque ruins were remarkable for creating an atmospheric beauty that, as we have seen, was rather lacking in the Forum itself, as recorded by him in 1636.

A little later, Claudian romance inspired the landscaped

parks of eighteenth-century England. At Stowe, Buckinghamshire, an imposing rostral column was raised in 1748 to commemorate the hero Thomas Grenville, who had died in a naval battle in the previous year. This was based on the similar column of Gaius Duilius at the Rostra in the Forum, fitted with the beaks of ships which he had captured in his naval victory over the Carthaginians at Mylae in 260 BC. The Temple of Concord and Victory at Stowe had been begun in 1746 on the lines of Roman peripteral temples, with a six-columned portico like that of the Temple of Vespasian and of the Temple of Antoninus and Faustina. It is not always appreciated that this ambitious temple at Stowe, perhaps designed by Thomas Grenville's brother, Lord Temple, is a major monument in western architecture, for it is probably the earliest full re-creation of a Roman temple.

In the meantime, this informed interest in Rome and the monuments in the Forum had helped inspire the creation by Louis XIV of the Académie Française in Rome in 1666 and of the Académie Royale d'Architecture five years later. His first minister, Jean-Baptiste Colbert, sent the young architect and scholar Antoine Desgodetz to Rome to make measured drawings. These would not only serve as a new and reliable record but would enable architectural students at the Royal Academy to learn from the best antique buildings without needing to travel to Rome. Desgodetz's drawings of 1676–7, including the principal monuments in the Forum, were published as beautiful copper-plate engravings in his *Les édifices antiques de Rome* (1682). These surpassed Palladio's woodcuts in accuracy, while the book, translated into English in two volumes in 1771 and 1795, remained the standard record until well into the nineteenth century, and is still extremely useful today.

Piranesi's images of the Forum as the Campo Vaccino, which we found helpful as a guide in Chapter 2, were echoed by many writers, for example Samuel Sharp, who recorded in his vituperative *Letters from Italy* (1766) that 'every Thursday and Friday a market for cows and oxen [is held] on the very spot where the Roman orators were accustomed to thunder out their eloquence in the cause of their clients, their country, and their gods.' Such musing on past oratory went back, as we have seen, to Poggio Bracciolini in the fifteenth century. James Boswell, biographer of Dr Johnson, similarly wrote in 1765, 'We viewed the celebrated Forum. I experienced sublime and melancholy emotions as I thought of all the great affairs which had taken place there, and saw the place now all in ruins with the wretched huts of carpenters and other artisans occupying the site of that rostrum from which Cicero had flung forth his stunning eloquence.'

The usual popular response of the eighteenth century to the Forum, this was even echoed by the great historian Edward Gibbon who, like Boswell, wrote of the 'several days of intoxication' when he first 'trod with a lofty step [in] the ruins of the Forum', adding that, 'each memorable spot where Romulus stood, or Tully [Cicero] spoke, or Caesar fell, was at once present to my eye.' In fact, it was wishful thinking that Caesar was assassinated in the Forum, for it was some distance away in the Portico of Pompey: the confusion arose from the fact that the Senate sometimes met, as on that fatal day, in an annexe attached to the Portico of Pompey.

Gibbon expanded on his life-changing experience in his *History of the Decline and Fall of the Roman Empire* (1776), where he explained that 'It was at Rome, on the 15th of

October 1764, as I sat musing amid the ruins of the Capitol, while the barefooted friars were singing vespers in the temple of Jupiter, that the idea of writing the decline and fall of the city first started to my mind.' He erred once again, for these Franciscan friars were chanting their office in the church of S. Maria in Aracoeli, built on the site of the Temple of Juno Moneta, pagan goddess of fortune. The great Temple of Jupiter Capitolinus was on the other, south, side of the Capitol. Piranesi made the same mistake in the caption to his view looking towards the Aracoeli from the Arch of Septimius Severus.

Forced to overhear the friars while he was musing above the Forum, Gibbon recorded his resentment that Rome, after its fall, had become cluttered with convents and monasteries: 'the number of these pious foundations was enormously multiplied; and the city was crowded with forty monasteries of men, twenty of women, and sixty chapters and colleges of canons and priests, who aggravated, instead of relieving, the depopulation of the tenth century.' In his polysyllabic if well-balanced prose, he further revealed the passionate anti-Catholicism of a lapsed Catholic convert by revealing how he saw a convent as no better than a stable: 'But if the forms of ancient architecture were disregarded by a people insensible of their use and beauty, the pitiful materials were applied to every call of necessity or superstition; till the fairest columns of the Ionic and Corinthian orders, the richest marble of Paros and Numidia, were degraded, perhaps to the support of a convent or a stable.'

Rational and modern though Gibbon doubtless imagined he was in comparing a nun to a horse, the age of Enlightenment in which he lived was about to demote his beloved

Rome as part of its insistence on the need to return to primary sources. Architecturally this meant Greece, not Rome. The great promoter of Greece, though he had never been there, was Johann Joachim Winckelmann (1717–68), the father of modern art history. He claimed in 1755 that 'The only way for us to become great, and if possible inimitable, lies in the imitation of the Greeks.' This was because Roman art was seen as a necessarily debased imitation of an earlier and purer style. Nonetheless, the pull of antiquarianism and hence of Rome was so great that Winckelmann left Germany in 1755 and moved south to Rome, where he was rewarded with his appointment as Prefect of Antiquities at the Vatican in 1763. In his capacity as librarian to the great collector Cardinal Albani, he seems to have had a hand in the creation of the ruined temple in the garden at the Villa Albani on the edge of Rome. This ruin survives as an evocation of the Roman Forum in a garden of antiquities.

A version in Polish of Winckelmann's great work, *History of the Art of the Ancients* (1764), was published with a commentary as *The Art of the Ancients, or Polish Winckelmann* by Count Stanislas Potocki, historian, collector, antiquarian and amateur architect. While in Rome in 1779–80, his reading of Winckelmann had led him to commission a vast restoration on paper of the Laurentine Villa of the younger Pliny. These drawings included a circular domed saloon with a rich frieze based on that of the Temple of Antoninus and Faustina in the Forum. A telling expression of the growing desire to replace romantic speculation with physical excavation is the reaction of Horace Walpole to Joseph Addison's *Remarks on Several Parts of Italy* (1705), a book which had been absorbed by countless Grand Tourists. Walpole complained in 1740 that

Addison had 'travelled through the poets and not through Italy; for all his ideas are borrowed from the descriptions and not from reality'.

In the Basilica Julia in 1788 the Swedish Ambassador, Carl Fredrik Fredenheim, may be said to have launched the first ever modern dig in the Forum. A follower of Winckelmann, he was an art historian and archaeologist, the Superintendant of the Royal Works and first Director of the Swedish Royal Museum. He helped form a collection of antiquities in Rome in the 1780s for King Gustav III of Sweden, which included diamond-shaped pieces of coloured marble. He brought these back from the Forum and incorporated them into a white marble table-top, proudly inscribed in gilt Trajan capitals on the front, E FUNDO FORI ROMANI MDCCLXXXIX ('From the depths of the Roman Forum, 1789'). This survives at Ostana on the Baltic shore, the severely neo-classical country house built in the 1790s for Carl Fredenheim's daughter.

This brings us to the greatest British neo-classical architect Sir John Soane, for whose work Greece and Rome were the twin pillars. Every year he commemorated 18 March as the day in 1778 when he had set out for Rome. This was because he believed that his career had been made in Rome, not only by what he saw but by the contacts he made with key future patrons. He studied the Forum in detail, drawing Vignola's gateway from it to the Farnese Gardens, and noting that Palladio had incorrectly added a colonnaded forecourt to the Temple of Antoninus and Faustina. Doubtless on the recommendation of his master, George Dance, he measured the Temple of Castor and Pollux in the Forum, hiring a ladder for this purpose. The danger of such performances was shown two years later when a French student was killed while measuring the Temple of Antoninus and Faustina in 1780.

Following Soane's appointment as Professor of Architecture at the Royal Academy in 1806, he commissioned his pupil Henry Parke to make a fine watercolour of a student precariously perched on a ladder while measuring the Corinthian capital of the Temple of Castor and Pollux (fig. 33). This was to show to his pupils in his lectures as a vivid demonstration of his belief that 'art cannot go beyond the Corinthian'. Parke's drawing is idealised, for he showed the capital intact, not decayed as in reality, and with the entablature returned, also not the case in the actual ruin. Soane nonetheless observed that the capital of this temple is full of originality and peculiar grace; the effect of the caulicoli, entwined in each other, is uncommonly beautiful, and highly rational, while the playfulness of the ornaments rising between them and the volutes which support the abacus cannot be sufficiently praised. One lecture would not be too long to point out the beauties of the entire composition.

Soane had studied carefully the Senate House at Cambridge (1722–30), where James Gibbs had unusually adopted this version of the Corinthian capital, as he also did in his exactly contemporary church of St Martin-in-the-Fields in London. This capital was rarely imitated, because its complicated intertwining elements were difficult and expensive to carve. Soane's buildings are frequently resonant with memories of the buildings and ruins of Rome, particularly as evoked by Piranesi. His screen in the Lothbury Court of 1798 at the Bank of England seems like the colonnade of the Temple of Castor and Pollux thrown picturesquely across an open space. In the garden of his own house, Pitzhanger Manor,

33. *Temple of Castor and Pollux (drawn by Henry Parke, c. 1810).*
Commissioned by the architect John Soane, this drawing shows one of his
students with top hat and measuring rod, precariously mounting a ladder
to measure the sumptuous Corinthian capital with its unique intertwining
stalks. In the background is the Arch of Titus.

Ealing (1800–1803), he even built mock Roman ruins like the one he had seen at the Villa Albani. He acquired casts of the orders of the temples in the Forum which can still be seen in Sir John Soane's Museum, his house and museum in Lincoln's Inn Fields, a thrilling, three-dimensional recreation of the Grand Tour. Another example of the way in which the monuments of the Forum have been constantly woven into the history of later architecture is the imposing Town Hall at Birmingham, begun in 1832 from designs by Joseph Aloysius Hansom and Edward Welch, who took as their model the entire Temple of Castor and Pollux in the Forum.

Soane was an acquaintance of William Beckford, possibly the greatest English collector of all time, with whom he shared a sense of being persecuted by the world. Beckford had been sent abroad by his mother at the age of twenty in 1780 in the hope that he would overcome his love-affair with the young William Courtenay. Arriving in Rome in October, a few months after Soane had left, his reactions show how his expectations, like those of Soane and countless others, had been coloured by the visionary Picturesque images of Piranesi. He thus recorded of the Pantheon that he 'began to think that Piranesi and Paolo Panini had been a great deal too colossal in their view of this venerable structure'. At the Forum next day:

*directing my steps to the arch of Constantine, I surveyed the groups of ruins which surrounded me. The cool breeze of the evening played in the beds of canes and osiers which flourished under the walls of the Coliseo ... I traversed the Campo Vaccino, and leaned a moment against one of the columns which supported the Temple of Jupiter Stator. Some women were fetching water from the fountain hard by, whilst another group had kindled a fire under the shrubs and twisted fig-trees which cover the Palatine hill. Innumerable vaults and arches peep out of the vegetation.*

Though Beckford found his tour aesthetically satisfying, it hardly fulfilled his mother's expectations, for his continuing relations with Courtenay were exposed in 1784 and he was socially ostracised for the rest of his life. Two years later, Johann Wolfgang von Goethe, the great polymath and man of letters, himself on the verge of an emotional breakdown, set off for Rome. Sometimes described as the last universal man, he was desperate to escape from his life as a court official in the small city of Weimar. Like Beckford, he was an intense romantic, obsessed with self and famous as the author of *The Sorrows of Young Werther* (1774), of which, as the story of a hypersensitive outsider, Beckford was a passionate admirer.

However, influenced by Winckelmann's call for calmness and simplicity in art and architecture, Goethe determined to visit Rome and Italy to study classicism at its source. His longing to reach 'classic soil' was so great that he dared not read the classics because they upset him so much. In 1786 he assumed the name of Möller and jumped into a coach with no servant and barely any luggage, exclaiming on arrival in Rome, 'Now, at last, I have arrived in the First City of the world!' He tried to follow Winckelmann in distinguishing the history of styles, but found in Rome that, for this purpose, 'Little spade-work has been done … A special training of the eye over many years would be required.' Envisaging himself musing in the Via Sacra in the Forum, surrounded by living history, Goethe explained that, here,

*One is, so to speak, reborn, and one's former ideas seem like a child's swaddling clothes. Here the most ordinary person becomes somebody ... Everywhere else one starts from the outside and works inward; here it seems to be the other way round. All history is encamped about us and all history sets forth again from us. This does not apply only to Roman history, but to the history of the whole world. From here I can accompany the conquerors to the Weser and the Euphrates, or, if I prefer to stand and gape, I can wait in the Via Sacra for their triumphant return.*

He finally quotes Winckelman's words: 'I believe that Rome is the school for the whole world, and I, too, have been purged and tested here.'

# 6

.............................................................................................

# FROM BYRON TO
# KING VICTOR EMMANUEL

So long as the Forum remained unexcavated, as in the eighteenth century, visitors could feel free to relax and absorb its picturesque if melancholy atmosphere. Contemplating the vanity of human wishes, they watched the cattle browsing over the ruins which were blissfully buried by grass and soil as though under drifts of snow or sand. This was still the world in which Byron wrote in *Childe Harold* in 1812,

> in yon field below
> A thousand years of silenced factions – sleep
> The Forum, where the immortal accents glow,
> And still the eloquent air breathes – burns with Cicero!

However, after archaeological investigation under the popes and the French from around 1800, visitors were told to study and instruct themselves before visiting the site, rather than see it as a place for sleep interrupted by vague dreams of Cicero. In the increasingly solemn world of Victorian England, this became a kind of penitential preparation, akin to prayer and fasting before a pilgrimage. Travellers turned for instruction to the most widely read Italian guidebook of the nineteenth century, Murray's *Handbook to Central Italy*, Part II, *Rome and its Environs*, first published in 1843. In an attempt to encourage visitors who were confronted by the challenge of a visit to the Forum, it told them in the edition of 1856 that, until now, 'the disputes of the antiquaries had involved every ruin in uncertainty, and had either bewildered the traveller into total scepticism, or made him believe that the sole interest of each object of antiquity consisted in the contest for its name.'

In the hope of relieving such bewilderment, visitors were informed in Murray's *Handbook* that 'the late Professor Nibby's *Roma Moderna*, in 2 vols. 8vo, 1839, will perhaps be found the most detailed and accurate description ... His *Mure di Roma* and *Foro Romano* and *Roma Antica* will well repay a perusal.' *The Indicazione Topografica di Roma Antica, del Commendatore Luigi Canina* (1850) was also welcomed, but a tart and donnish tone now entered: 'Robello's *Guide de Rome* ... is full of errors, and written in a disagreeably pedantic style.' So why mention it? Worse, it was complained that in the '*Beschreibung von Stadt Rome*, 5 vols. 8vo. and *Atlas*, 1830–1842 by Bunsen, Plattner, Rostell, Gehrard, Uhlrichs, &c. ... a series of separate incompletely connected dissertations, render its perusal unsatisfactory, and detract from its merit as a guide', while its authors' habit of frequently challenging the opinions of previous writers 'in unsettling the mind of the visitor, takes away much of his interest in the scenes of classical antiquity with which he is surrounded'. As though this were insufficiently off-putting, readers were warned that 'The few plates with which the *Beschreibung* is accompanied are copied from other works, and are too few for its illustration.'

It was also dispiriting, if accurate, to find in Murray's *Handbook* that 'it is impossible to define exactly the limits of the Forum and its dimensions'. The plan provided, taken from that by Luigi Canina, was thus largely blank: the Basilica Aemilia was scarcely included, and misidentified as S. Adriano; the Forum ended with the temple of Antoninus and Faustina; while there was, of course, nothing on the as yet unexcavated Temple of Vesta or House of the Vestals. Thus, in a book of 356 pages, the entire Forum was despatched in four pages, the same number as were allocated to a single monument, the ever popular Colosseum.

Even Dr Thomas Arnold, the great headmaster of Rugby, a brilliant classical scholar and author of an uncompleted *History of Rome* (1838–42), described the Forum to his wife in 1840 as a 'scene of desolation', declaring impatiently, 'What the fragments of pillars belonged to, perhaps we can never know; but I think that matters little. I care not whether it was a temple of Jupiter Stator or the Basilica Julia.' What counted most for him was the larger picture: 'one knows that one is on the ground of the Forum, under the Capitol, the place where the tribes assembled and the orators spoke: the scene, in short, of all the internal struggles of the Roman people.'

Similarly, George Stillman Hillard, the Boston lawyer and friend of Nathaniel Hawthorne, observed in 1853 that the great British architect and archaeologist C. R. Cockerell 'has published a print which he calls the Restoration of the Forum … but on the spot I could never recall the past'. He also referred to the countless guilty visitors to Rome who returned 'haunted by visions of churches that had not been seen and galleries that had not been visited'. Faced with such adversity, some guidebooks nourished their readers with a kind of comfort food by describing Rome in the familiar terms of English topography, one of the more improbable parallels being Augustus Hare's claim that 'The Campagna [is] rather like the Bagshot Heath country.' In Murray's *Handbook*, the Forum, in its phase as the Campo Vaccino, was 'a kind of Roman Smithfield', while F. M. Nichols, in his serious monograph on the Forum of 1877, brought it to life by describing how 'The same area which was the Westminster Hall, the Old Bailey and the Tower Hill, was also the Lombard Street and the Exchange of Rome.' He suggested that the Mamertine prison 'plays a part in Roman history like that of the Tower of London in English … a Secret Tower Hill … [which] like the Tower, had also its literary reminiscences. Naevius is said to have written two of his plays while confined in the prison for his attacks on the aristocracy.' A late example of these reassuring domestic analogies is in Dudley's excellent book *Urbs Roma* (1967), where, in an echo of the game of Monopoly, Virgil's reference in the *Aeneid* to 'wealthy Carinae', with its cattle, is seen as the equivalent of Park Lane.

In 1868, the German archaeologist Heinrich Schliemann relied heavily while in Italy on the John Murray *Handbook of Rome and Its Environs*. Even more significantly, he used in his discoveries at Troy and Mycenae Murray's *Handbook for Travellers to Greece* as the inspiration for his Homeric itinerary. Augustus Hare, in his popular two-volumed *Walks in Rome*, first published in 1871, recommended that visitors should spend eleven full days in the city, but in the list of what they should see each day, 'the Forum in detail' was left until the afternoon of the penultimate day. Murray's *Handbook* warned that 'Shoes and boots are dear in Rome, and indifferent, especially against wet,' and that the English church was closed from June to October. On the plus side, although pavements, except in the Corso, were lit only with oil lamps, a few in the last two years 'have been lighted with gas, as ultimately the entire city will be, thanks to an English company, who have erected a very extensive gas works on the site of the Circus Maximus'. Perhaps the Forum had been rejected as too small for this purpose.

Hare complained that beggars were 'encouraged by the Municipality and persecute foreigners even in the churches … Maimed limbs and borrowed children are everywhere exhibited with impunity.' On the other hand, 'Trattorie send out dinners to families in apartments in a tin box with a stove, for which the bearer calls the next morning. A dinner for six francs ought to be sufficient for three persons, and to leave enough for lunch on the next day.' Also, 'Foxhounds meet twice a week in the Campagna. The meets are posted at Piale's Library. Throw off at 11.'

The great historian and East India Company administrator Lord Macaulay had anticipated Hare and Nichols' comparison of Rome and the Forum to English places and institutions. In a review of Leopold von Ranke's *History of the Popes*, Macaulay suggested that 'The Capitol and the Forum impress us with less awe than our own Westminster Hall and Westminster Abbey.' This was no cheap attempt to downplay the Forum, for it was precisely the extent to which Macaulay valued Roman civilisation that enabled him to judge the merit which Britain had attained by equalling it. He was thus the heir to the eighteenth-century writers who saw themselves as Augustan.

In his widely read poem 'The Battle of the Lake Regillus' in *Lays of Ancient Rome* (1842), Macaulay celebrated the Temple of Castor and Pollux in the Forum as 'a stately dome', perhaps echoing the language of Coleridge's *Kubla Khan* (1816). As we have seen, the temple had been founded near the spot where the two semi-mystical cavalry heroes, Castor and his twin brother Pollux, had announced the Roman victory at Lake Regillus in the early fifth century BC. Macaulay will have known Cicero's praise of the temple as 'the famous and glorious monument of the past, that sanctuary which stands where the eyes of the nation may rest on it every day'. The association of Castor and Pollux with a ritual order of knights even led Macaulay to compare them for the benefit of modern readers to the medieval English order of the Knights of the Garter. It is in such a context that we should see Macaulay's romantic understanding of the Catholic Church as the heir to the Roman empire:

> *The history of that Church joins together the two great ages of human civilisation. No other institution is left standing which carries the mind back to the times when the smoke of sacrifice rose from the Pantheon, and when camelopards and tigers bounded in the Flavian amphitheatre.*

Macaulay's Victorian blend of classics and Anglicanism is well conveyed by the Reverend William Selwyn, Lady Margaret Professor of Divinity at Cambridge, who was happy to compare King's College Chapel to the great Temple of Jupiter Capitolinus in Rome. This was in a speech in the Senate House in 1875 when, urging the building of a new Divinity School, in the Gothic style, near King's Chapel, he said that the Chapel 'will be seen high above it, as the Capitol of Rome is seen high above the Temples in the Forum'.

The identification of the British with the Roman Empire was expressed in the 1850s by Lady Eastlake, who felt at the Colosseum that 'my nation is the descendant of the matchless race', and by the American George Stillman Hillard, who simply stated that the British were 'the legitimate descendants of the old Romans, the true inheritors of their spirit'. He sketched a vivid picture of how 'They stalk over the land as if it were their own,' though such a view was normally combined with a more anti-Catholic outlook than that of Macaulay. Conforming to the view that everyone finds in Rome what they want to find, Charles Dickens was preoccupied on his visit to the Forum by the Colosseum as a dramatic evocation of horror. He recalled how,

> The ghostly pillars in the Forum; the Triumphal Arches of Old Emperors; those enormous masses of ruin which were once their palaces; the grass-grown mounds that mark the graves of ruined temples; the stones of the Via Sacra … even these were dimmed, in their transcendent melancholy, by the dark ghost of its bloody holidays, erect and grim [the Colosseum].

At the other end of the Forum, it was inevitably the Mamertine prison that gripped Dickens: 'the dread and gloom of the ponderous, obdurate old prison are on it, as though they had come up from a dark mist through the floor,' like the sinister Kent marshes in the opening of *Great Expectations* (1861). He was excited to find in the prison that,

> Hanging on the walls … are objects, at once strangely in keeping, and strangely at variance, with the place – rusty daggers, knives, pistol, clubs, divers instruments of violence and murder brought

*here, fresh from use, and hung up to propitiate offended Heaven:*
*as if the blood upon them would drain off in consecrated air.*

At this point, it is hard to follow the seemingly drugged mind of Dickens that led him to write how 'this little dark spot becomes a dream within a dream: and in the vision of great churches which come rolling past me like a sea, it is a small wave by itself, that melts into another wave, and does not flow on with the rest.'

By the mid-nineteenth century, the decay in the Forum, which had exercised such a nostalgic appeal to the minds of men as different as Piranesi and Gibbon, was considered unsightly and depressing by visitors from North America as well as from England. Thus, George Stillman Hillard complained in 1853 that,

*no one unless forewarned by books and engravings, can have any conception of the change and desolation which have overcome this neglected spot. An unsightly piece of ground, disfeatured with filth and neglect, with a few ruins scattered over it, and two formal rows of trees ... A few peasants wrapped in their mud-coloured cloaks, a donkey or two, a yoke of the fine gray oxen of Italy ... are the only living forms in a scene once peopled with wisdom, valor, and eloquence.*

In 1866, William Dean Howells was similarly put off by what he saw as a 'dirty cowfield, wandered over by evil-eyed buffaloes and obscenely defiled by wild beasts', with the ancient ruins sometimes 'half-gorged by the façade of a hideous Renaissance church'.

However, since so little survives of the Forum, every visitor can interpret it with his own romantic imagination. Less than a generation after down-to-earth visitors like Hillard and Howells, Walter Pater published his languid aesthetic romance, *Marius the Epicurean* (1885), an essay in refined sensuality woven round Roman religion and philosophy. With his close friend Cornelius, Marius visits the Forum on his first day in Rome where the two young men find that,

> *The Temple of Antoninus and Faustina was still fresh in all the majesty of its closely arrayed columns of* cipollino; *but, on the whole, little had been added under the late and present emperors, and during fifty years of public quiet, a sober brown and gray had grown apace on things.*

Interpreting Rome as the home of dreaming spires and lost causes, the Oxford of the Roman Empire, Pater presents Marius as a man who, having studied Plato's *Phaedrus*, 'must be made perfect by the love of visible beauty'. Pater explains that when Marius arrives in the Rome of the Antonines in the second century AD, 'Much which spoke of ages earlier than Nero, the great re-builder, lingered on, antique, quaint, immeasurably venerable, like the relics of the medieval city in the Paris of Lewis the Fourteenth.' Marius subsequently goes to the Forum to listen to Emperor Marcus Aurelius addressing the Senators 'in the vast hall of the Curia Julia', where he is struck by 'The antique character of their attire' and by their curule chairs which, Pater cannot help adding, are like those 'still in use in the Roman church when a Bishop pontificates at the divine offices'. In a vision in which he looks both back to archaic Rome and forwards to the fall of the Empire, Marius 'seemed to foresee a grass-grown Forum, the broken ways of the Capitol, and the Palatine hill itself in humble occupation'. Pater had in mind Virgil's *Aeneid*, in which, as we saw in Chapter I, the Arcadian king Evander, taking Aeneas to the place where the city of Rome would one day stand, 'approached the dwelling of the humble Evander, and they saw the cattle everywhere, lowing in the Forum of Rome'.

Pater describes how the Temple of Peace, next to the Forum, 'enlarged by a library and lecture rooms, had grown into an institution like something between a college and a literary club', in fact reassuringly like Balliol College, Oxford, of which Pater was a Fellow. In this proto-Oxonian setting, peopled by clever and attractive young men, Marius listens to a discourse on the Nature of Morals, after which he goes into the Forum to see the procession of the military knights of Castor and Pollux, earlier admired by Macaulay. On another occasion in the Forum, 'The two friends descended along the Vicus Tuscus, with its rows of incense stalls, into the Via Nova, where the fashionable people were busy shopping.' They also visit the flower-market and, 'Loitering to the other side of the Forum, past the great Galen's drug-shop, after a glance at the announcements of new poems on sale attached to the doorpost of a famous bookseller, they entered the curious library of the Temple of Peace', a favourite haunt of Pater in his dreams. He goes on to describe how

> *Twelve o'clock was come before they left the Forum, waiting in a little crowd to hear the* Accensus, *according to an old custom, proclaim the hour of noonday, at the moment when, from the steps of the Senate-house, the sun could be seen standing between the* Rostra *and the* Graecostasis.

Napoleon invaded the Papal States in 1797, his forces entering Rome on 10 February 1798. A short-lived Roman Republic was set up that was so modern, i.e. neo-antique, in character that it had to be centred on the Forum. Five days after French troops entered Rome, the Republican followers marched along the Corso to the Forum where, following recent practice in Revolutionary festivals in France, a great tree of liberty, prepared previously, was planted by the Arch of Septimius Severus. Duke Braschi, the Pope's nephew, laid a garland at its foot. Antonio Bassi, shortly to become a Consul in the Roman Republic, mounted a fallen column and harangued the assembled Republicans, urging them to overthrow the papacy and abolish all emblems of oppression. The old scaffolds which stood in the Forum and in three squares as a warning to criminals were torn down as relics of barbarism. A Roman newspaper observed of the Forum that,

> *After centuries of decay and neglect, the site thus recovered its original civic function as a gathering place 'for the people and the Senate when it became necessary to deliberate on the gravest concerns of the Republic.'*

This ceremony, aimed at shifting the seat of authority from the Vatican to the Forum, was designed to upstage a ceremony which was held at St Peter's that day to celebrate the twenty-third anniversary of the election to the papacy of Pius VI. The triumph of the Republic was complete, for the Pope was shortly taken prisoner by the French and died in exile at Valence in August 1799.

In February 1799, to celebrate the anniversary of the Republic, another festival was held in the Forum, in which a giant temporary Doric column, surmounted by a statue of liberty, was set up in front of S. Lorenzo in Miranda (Temple of Antoninus and Faustina). Throughout Rome, Republican symbols displaced Christian ones, streets and piazzas were given new names, convents were suppressed, and the Jews released from the Ghetto, where they had been confined since its establishment by Pope Paul IV in 1555 along the lines of those in Venice and Prague. However, late in 1799, Neapolitan forces invaded Rome and destroyed all souvenirs of the twenty-month Republican regime. Moreover, in the following July, Pope Pius VII, newly elected in Venice, returned in a triumphant procession to the Vatican to begin his long reign of twenty-three years, during which he was successful in restoring the prestige of the papacy. He found the Vatican stripped of its iconic works of art and its museums dismantled, Napoleon having carted away to the Louvre hundreds of the finest sculptures and paintings. 'Rome is no longer in Rome,' Napoleon boasted, 'The whole of Rome is in Paris.'

Pius VII and his right-hand man, Cardinal Ercole Consalvi, his Secretary of State (prime minister) throughout his reign, saw it as important to the image of the papacy to retrieve the works of art from Paris, to restore the monuments of ancient Rome, and to reinstate the authority of the church. It was Consalvi who negotiated the terms of the Concordats of 1801 and 1803 in which Napoleon respectively restored the Catholic religion in France and confirmed that the Catholic Church was the state religion in Italy. It was also Consalvi who appointed the lawyer and antiquarian Carlo Fea as archaeological director of the Forum in 1803, with the aim of excavating and repairing the ancient monuments. In fact, Fea had already been appointed Commissioner for Roman Antiquities in 1799 by the occupying Neapolitan general, Naselli. The traveller and wit Lord Glenbervie, who was in Rome in 1815–16, described Fea as 'splenetic and satirical', while Cardinal Nicholas Wiseman saw him as happier seeking knowledge in a library than 'digging in the earth'. Indeed, Fea translated Winckelmann's *History of Ancient Art* and published many books on Rome.

In 1803, the Pope promoted an Edict for protecting the Roman antiquities and appointed the great sculptor Antonio Canova as Inspector General of Antiquities and Fine Arts in the States of the Church and Curator of the Vatican and Capitoline Museums. Canova commissioned a series of paintings in lunettes in the Galleria Chiaramonti in the Vatican depicting aspects of Pius VII's patronage of artists and archaeologists. The central lunette, by Vincenzo Ferreri, shows the seated Pope unexpectedly handing the Edict to a small male angel with long hair and very large wings, and in another scene he is shown visiting his excavations in the Forum. His activity as a collector was partly a reaction to the decimation by Napoleon of the papal collections, while the excavation of the triumphal arches of Septimius Severus and of Constantine could be seen as a statement of renewed papal power and wealth, in contrast to the short-lived Republican regime under Napoleon, which celebrated its triumphs with ephemeral arches and columns of wood and canvas.

In May 1809, following the occupation of Rome by French forces in the previous year, Napoleon declared that the Papal States were now part of his Empire, with Rome as its second city after Paris. The kidnapping and deportation of the Pope by the French on the night of 6 July 1809 shocked both Catholics and Protestants throughout Europe, Napoleon losing much political sympathy by turning a frail man into a martyr. However, even though Pius VII did not return to Rome until May 1814, his absence made little difference to the history of the Forum, because Napoleon wisely reappointed most of the papal architects and archaeological advisers, including Fea, Canova, Giuseppe Valadier, Raffaello Stern and Filippo Aurelio Visconti. Indeed, in a move which would have been condemned as 'collaboration' in France in the 1940s, many Roman aristocrats and members of the upper bourgeoisie and commercial classes, as well as architects, supported the French, who rewarded them with office and commissions. Also, though supposedly the second city of the French empire, Rome never had a governor, the civil head being the Prefect of the Department of Rome, Count Camille de Tournon (1778–1833). A humane and cultivated man, he arrived in November 1809 and left in January 1814.

The Forum, remarkably, was thus seen as an appropriate arena for the expression of power by the Italian pope and the French emperor alike. In fact, Napoleon never visited Rome. After all, he hardly needed to, for he had created a sumptuous version of the Arch of Septimius Severus in the form of the Arc du Carrousel, built by Percier and Fontaine in 1806–8 in front of his Paris residence, the former Bourbon palace of the Tuileries. But seeing a chance to win glory, a Roman architect, Scipione Perosini, hoped to entice Napoleon with his plans of 1811 for an imperial palace on a megalomaniac scale, running from the Piazza Colonna in the Corso to the Colosseum. With its innumerable porticoes, galleries and marble staircases, this was to incorporate the Palazzo Venezia as its administrative wing, the historic church of S. Maria Aracoeli on the Capitol as its chapel, and the Forum as its inner courtyard! Before dismissing this as fantasy, we should note that in the same year Napoleon commissioned Percier and Fontaine to design the Palais de Chaillot as a residence for his new-born son, Napoléon François Joseph Charles (1811–32), whom he named the King of Rome and who became titular Napoleon II for a short period in 1814. The proposed Palais de Chaillot, a neo-classical Versailles that would have occupied a vast area of central Paris, remained an unrealised dream.

In the meantime, Tournon tried to make Rome sufficiently magnificent for a proposed visit to the second imperial city by Napoleon and his new wife, Empress Marie-Louise, whom Napoleon had married in April 1810. Describing the ground in the Forum as four metres above the ancient level, and as many as ten at the foot of Capitol, Tournon hired over 2,000 workers to clear the rubble, beginning with the Tabularium and Temple of Vespasian. Though the visit did not take place, the archaeological preparations were put to good use one night in June 1811 when each monument in the Forum between and including the Colosseum and the Capitol was illuminated to celebrate the birth in March of Napoleon's son. Watched by a vast crowd, this early attempt at a *son et lumière* performance was perhaps the first such use of an archaeological setting as a kind of propagandist window-dressing. At the same time, the celebrations included the characteristic trappings of the festivals of *ancien régime* monarchies, including a *Te Deum* at St Peter's, ill-attended, a banquet and a ball. The very title 'King of Rome' was that which was traditionally borne by the heir of the Holy Roman

Emperor, even though Napoleon had abolished this office with the Holy Roman Empire in 1806.

In 1811 another striking and visionary approach to the ancient buildings in the Forum aimed at framing them with clumps of trees and linking them, where appropriate, with lawns. Known as 'Le Jardin du Capitol', this Napoleonic tribute to the English taste for Picturesque landscape was drawn up in January 1811 by two papal architects, Giuseppe Camporese and Giuseppe Valadier. Their unexecuted landscaped proposal has been variously interpreted: the right-wing French architectural historian Louis Hautecoeur hailed it as 'already the idea of the "Passeggiata archaeologica" which was realised by the Fascist government', while Christopher Woodward sees it as 'the final triumph of English tourists' claim to understand Rome better than the Romans'. Plans for a giant formal garden on the Palatine linked to a more modest garden in the Forum were prepared in 1813 by Louis-Martin Berthault, who had designed gardens for the Empress Josephine at Malmaison in 1805.

If Valadier, whose grandfather had migrated from France to Italy, was unable to create the Forum gardens, he was responsible for the celebrated gardens on the Pincian Hill above the Piazza del Popolo, which he laid out for Pius VII in 1816–24. These, however, were in a formal, not an English Picturesque, taste. Camporese, architect of the Pantheon-inspired Sale della Biga (1787–92) for Pius VI at the Museo Pio-Clementino in the Vatican, oversaw excavations in the Forum from 1810–13 and in Trajan's Forum from 1812–13. He was involved in the complex task of rebuilding the Temple of Vespasian in the Forum, of which more in a moment.

The combined proposals for restoring the monuments

and creating a garden involved the purchase and demolition of the numerous modern buildings in the Forum, a process scheduled to take between four and six years. The buildings that were demolished, many of a modest vernacular character, included granaries, sheds, haylofts, a foundry and barns, and houses owned by monasteries, by private individuals, and a few by the state. Not surprisingly, many objected to the drastic change of character brought about by this destruction. George Stillman Hillard, the American lawyer from whose best-selling *Six Months in Rome* we have already quoted, complained that the archaeologists, by dissecting the Forum like a corpse, had 'dug unsightly holes and opened deforming trenches' in it. They had thus succeeded in creating a scene of 'desolation which is not beautiful; a ruin which is not picturesque'.

The excavation of the Forum, lamented by Hillard, had been a continuous process under the popes and the occupying French. Fea explored the Forum for Pius VII from 1803–19, beginning by disinterring the Arch of Septimius Severus, using prisoners as labourers. In the process he demolished the surviving portion of SS. Sergio e Bacco al Foro, an early example of the unhappy destruction of churches in the Forum. It was also ironical, for the arch had been preserved because it belonged in part to the church.

Attention was now turned to the nearby Temple of Vespasian, thought to be that of Jupiter Tonans (the Thunderer) until its correct identification by Antonio Nibby after 1827. When excavation began in 1810, it was found that its three surviving columns had fallen out of the perpendicular by over two feet and were only supported by the accumulated earth. Indeed, rubbish and soil reached almost to the top of the column shafts, an effect vividly conveyed in a celebrated engraving by Piranesi (fig. 14). Tournon described how Valadier and Camporese dismantled the columns, re-erecting them on new foundations, so that the present steps and podium date from 1811. The archaeologist Rodolfo Lanciani fancifully claimed in 1897 that, when the soil was removed, 'the expectant public could see outlined against the sky those capitals and that frieze which, only a few months before, had been trodden by the feet of tourists'.

When the French had arrived, the free-standing Corinthian column near the Arch of Septimius Severus, now known to be the Column of Phocas, was hidden among houses, notably that of Duca Mattei (figs 1 and 6). These were demolished and the column excavated between 1811 and 1813. Its history and identity had been the subject of many guesses, so the discovery in 1813 of a dedicatory inscription on the north side of its marble pedestal was hailed with excitement when it was announced by the antiquarian Filippo Aurelio Visconti in June that year. It was now thought possible to identify the year of the erection of the column as AD 608, because according to the inscription it was originally surmounted by a statue of Emperor Phocas dedicated in that year.

A small role was now played in the excavation of the Column of Phocas by one of the more exotic creatures of the world of the Grand Tour who took up residence in Rome in 1814. This was Elizabeth, Duchess of Devonshire, who immediately began subsidising excavations in the Forum. Daughter of the eccentric collector and patron the Earl-Bishop of Derry, and successively the mistress, second wife and widow of the 5th Duke of Devonshire, she was adored by characters as varied as Edward Gibbon and Cardinal Consalvi. A patron of the arts and a hostess, she held court in the state apartments at the Palazzo Spada. Consalvi enabled her to excavate in the Forum near the Column of Phocas in 1816–17, where, with the help of manacled convicts, she found the pyramid of eleven marble steps on which the column rested.

Augustus Hare, ever a friend of duchesses, claimed absurdly that 'The excavations made in the forum before 1876 were for the most part due to the generosity of Elizabeth, Duchess of Devonshire,' while many up to the present day, dazzled by her wealth and aristocratic glamour, have attributed to her the discovery of the inscription and even of the column itself. Byron curiously referred to the Column of Phocas as 'Thou nameless column with a buried base' in 1817, four years after the identification of Phocas had given it a name. However, he may have found mystery more romantic than truth, for Phocas was a brutal centurion in the Byzantine army who had usurped the throne by massacring the emperor Maurice and his five sons. An even larger task was undertaken at the other end of the Forum when soil was removed for the excavation and restoration of the Basilica of Maxentius in 1811–24. Work was also carried out on the adjacent Temple of Venus and Roma in 1813–14.

Napoleon's glory was short-lived, for after his defeat at the Battle of Leipzig in 1813 he abdicated in 1814, in which year the Bourbon monarchy was restored in France. In the Forum, the work of Napoleon's restorers was halted, so that when Herman Friedlaender visited it in 1815–16 he found that the recently excavated monuments were already overgrown with ivy intertwined with violets and marigolds. It had reverted to a place of deep silence, with 'bulls and buffaloes, peaceably ruminating near their carts or wagons', interrupted only by 'monks creeping to their convents'.

After Cardinal Consalvi had managed to secure the restoration of the Papal States and temporal power at the Congress of Vienna, Pius VII returned triumphantly to Rome in 1814. He sought now to re-emphasise the role of the Colosseum as a shrine to Catholic martyrdom, filling in Camille de Tournon's excavations of 1813 which had made it less practical for that purpose, though, as Mary Beard has pointed out, 'there are no genuine records of any Christians being put to death in the Colosseum … No accounts of martyrdoms there are earlier than the fifth century AD, by which time Christianity had become the official religion of Rome'. Pius VII also returned the Jews to the Ghetto, where they remained until the walls were demolished under the Republic in 1848, though they were not given equal rights until 1870.

In 1819 he ordered the restoration of the Arch of Titus, which had long been offensive to Jews as a monument erected to commemorate their defeat and the destruction of the temple of Jerusalem in AD 70. They were not allowed to pass under it, though it was one of the monuments for which they were required to provide decorations on the occasion of the *possesso*, the procession of popes going to the Lateran for their coronation. The pope would halt at the Arch of Titus, where a Jew presented a copy of the Pentateuch with a humble oath of loyalty, a humiliating ceremony which some have claimed had ancient Roman origins.

We should realise that from the Middle Ages until the nineteenth century the appearance of the Arch of Titus was very different from how it looks today, for it had been immured in the Palatine defences erected by the Frangipane

34. *Arch of Titus, east front*. The whole of the side bays with their outer
columns and surmounting attic were newly built by Stern and Valadier who
deliberately used a different material for their work and omitted fluting from
the new columns.

family in the twelfth century. They had removed the whole of the side wings or pylons and had also added a top storey of brick, destroying the whole cornice. On the west front facing the Forum, the attic and its inscription had gone, as had the top half of the columns flanking the arch, together with their capitals. Its restoration, begun by Stern in 1819, was one of the most tricky jobs in the Forum, for the surviving central archway was propped up by later buildings, the demolition of which threatened its stability. Stern thus decided to dismantle it first and then to reassemble it. After his death in 1820 the task was completed in 1821–2 by Valadier, with far more new work than is realised by most visitors (fig. 34). He provided the whole of the side pylons, most of the attic, its cornice, and the large panel with the inscription on its east front recording the completion of its rebuilding by Pius VII in 1823.

Except for its figured sculptural panels, the Arch of Titus is thus today largely a nineteenth-century monument. Controversially, Stern and Valadier attempted to distinguish their work from the old by making their new side pylons in a simple neo-classical, rather than in an ancient Roman, style: for example, they priggishly replaced the missing Composite columns at the ends of the arch with columns without flutes, despite the fact that the originals had been fluted. They also built their new work in travertine rather than the Pentelic marble of the original. All this represented a very early victory of archaeology over art. The arch had originally been built in a single expensive material as a sophisticated and harmonious work of art, featuring one of the first examples of that characteristically Roman invention, the Composite order. But instead of presenting it as a monument with a visible unity, Stern and Valadier chose to celebrate the temporary practical skills of the restorer rather than the eternal vision of the original architect.

Such practices were nonetheless incorporated and developed in the Charter of Venice of 1964 which, with disastrous consequences, has since been universally adopted in the restoration of major historic buildings. The Charter insists that 'Replacement of missing parts must be distinguishable from the original so that restoration does not falsify the artistic or historic evidence', and that 'all reconstruction work must be ruled out *a priori*': in other words, Modernist architectural orthodoxy prevents a present-day architect from working in an historical language. As the architect Léon Krier complains, 'This leads to the preservation of honest fragments, rather than of masterpieces in their organic and organisational coherence.' It also ignores the fact that to survive with visual coherence, any ancient building needs restoration, including accurate replacement of decayed stonework, about once a century.

Valadier falsely claimed for himself all the credit for restoring the Arch of Titus in the book he published on the subject in 1822, but Stendhal (Henri Beyle) complained of him in 1828 that, 'He had the nerve to hew blocks of travertino after the form of the antique stones and to substitute them for these, which were carried away I know not where. What remains to us is therefore but a *copy* of Titus's arch.'

A final problem which the Arch of Titus shares with the 'Temple of Romulus' and the Basilica of Maxentius, is that, as Coarelli put it, they 'have ended up practically suspended in mid air, with their foundations uncovered'. This is because nineteenth-century archaeologists largely destroyed the post-Neronian pavement on which they stood, taking it to be a medieval addition. However, the Arch of Titus was admired in the nineteenth century and even influenced the bold addition of 1852–68 by Virgilio Vespignani to Michelangelo's Porta Pia in Rome. Such a fruitful interaction between antique, Renaissance and modern work is surely a message at the heart of the Roman experience, and one which visitors could be encouraged to carry away from the Forum; at the time of writing, they are not even allowed to walk through the Arch of Titus!

In 1827 Leo XII appointed Professor Antonio Nibby as director of excavations in the Forum in succession to his older rival, Fea. A prolific author of books on ancient Rome, Nibby furthered in-depth excavation, in opposition to Fea, as well as the demolition of modern buildings, clearing the northern part of the Forum at the Tabularium and Temple of Concord. He established for the first time that the smaller temple adjacent to the Temple of Concord was not that of Jupiter Tonans as had long been believed, but, as we have noted above, of the Emperor Vespasian. He also, against fierce opposition from Fea, concluded correctly that the great building at the other end of the Forum, known since the fifteenth century as the Temple of Peace, was in fact the Basilica of Maxentius. In 1827–9, he completely cleared the adjacent Temple of Venus and Roma, where, as we have seen, excavations had begun in 1813–14. He discovered the brick stamps which confirmed its Hadrianic date.

King Ludwig I of Bavaria, who rebuilt Munich as a neo-classical and Romantic city from 1825–48 and was also a passionate collector of antique, especially Greek, sculpture, was surprisingly hostile to the recent activities of the archaeologists in the Forum. He observed of it scathingly in 1834,

'Artists have nothing to say, archaeologists rule as they please here, blind to all, caring for nought but their own.'

In 1839 Nibby was succeeded as Commissario alle Antichità by the distinguished architect and architectural historian Luigi Canina, who worked systematically from 1848–53, partially excavating the Basilica Julia in 1835 and 1848. His work in the basilica was noted without enthusiasm by Nathaniel Hawthorne, who spent the years 1858–60 in Italy, where his experiences as an American in Europe led to his novel *The Marble Faun* (1860), which was later to inspire Henry James. He described how he 'went down into the excavations' in the Forum, where he found the Basilica Julia to be 'heaps of bricks, shapeless bits of marble and granite, and other ancient rubbish'. An even more disagreeable sight was the evidence of frequent defecation which he found all over the Forum; he had to step with particular care under the Arch of Titus. He was amused, by contrast, to discover that in the vicinity of ruins the Romans were 'addicted to washing of clothes' so that sheets flapped all round the Forum 'wherever … an iron railing affords an opportunity to hang them.'

Nonetheless, he noted that in March 1859 as many as 1,500 American visitors were reported to be in Rome. Indeed, the 1850s marked the flood tide of Americans in Italy, though poets such as Browning, Coventry Patmore and Arthur Hugh Clough, as well as novelists such as Dickens and Thackeray, felt that they had overlooked the squalor of Rome in their veneration for its history and its ruins.

One striking consequence of the serious interest of the French in the monuments of ancient Rome and of the Forum in particular is the stunning series of restoration drawings by French architectural students who had won the Grand Prix

35. *Meta Sudans, Arch of Titus, Temple of Venus and Roma, Colossus of Nero, and Basilica of Maxentius, from the east (restoration drawing by E.-G. Coquart, 1863).* One of the most vivid recreations of the overwhelming splendour of imperial Rome. On the left is the Meta Sudans, a monumental conical fountain of *c.* AD 89 which was demolished under Mussolini in 1936.

of the Académie Royale d'Architecture and its successor, the École des Beaux-Arts, in Paris (figs 17 and 35). This qualified them to spend a period of study at the Académie Française de Rome (still surviving today at the Villa Medici) with the obligation to send back a reconstruction of an ancient monument at the end of their third year. This process reached a climax in the first three quarters of the nineteenth century, when the young architects studied the work of archaeologists such as Nibby, producing beautifully detailed 'before and after' watercolours of the monuments in the Forum.

However, some of the young architectural students, anxious to begin designing real buildings, rebelled against this programme, because by the 1860s they saw it as a product of the positivist and scientific approach that was replacing the traditional humanist architect-archaeologist with the professional archaeologist and engineer. Describing in 1867 his attempt to reconstruct an ancient monument, Julien Guadet (1834–1908) confessed, 'I can say I did the best I could; yet I did so reluctantly,' adding, 'What were forums, basilicas, libraries, or temples meant to be? I cannot say.' He argued that to reconstruct them 'is as absurd as a modern writer who, however distinguished a Latin expert he may be, sets about to reconstruct the missing parts of Cicero and Tacitus.'

The skills of Julien Guadet, who summarised his position in a brief aphorism, 'Archaeology is the enemy', lay not as a practising architect but as a teacher and theorist, expressed in his four-volume *Eléments et théorie de l'architecture* (1901–4). More gifted architects such as his master Labrouste, as well as Hittorff, Vignon, Duc, Vaudoyer and Nénot, were able to put the Beaux-Arts reconstructions of monumental Roman works to imaginative use in their powerful public buildings in nineteenth-century Paris and other French cities.

## ARCHAEOLOGISTS UNDER THE KINGS OF UNITED ITALY

Following the year of revolution in Europe, 1848, a Republic was set up in Rome itself and Pius IX briefly deposed. He was rescued by Emperor Napoleon III, but though the Republic lasted from only 1849 to 1850, it found time to prepare a vast plan of excavations in the Forum. The democrats sought to discover an authentic Republican tradition in Italy in the belief that excavation would promote civic and national ideals. This was in contrast to papal promotion of the idea that there was a providential continuity between Classical and Christian Rome. Such a notion may have inspired the rebuilding of the Portico of the Harmonious Gods by Pius IX in 1858, the last major papal intervention in the Forum (fig. 18).

However, Italy had seen the beginning of a process of national unification in 1861, and Rome was declared capital of the new country on 3 February 1871 under a new monarchy, the House of Savoy. From September 1870, when Piedmontese forces finally entered Rome to wrest it from papal control, the process of transforming it into the modern capital of the new united Italy was undertaken with astonishing speed. With the building of new government buildings, transport networks and residential quarters, not aimed at *savants* and nobles, the population, barely 250,000 in 1870, doubled within twenty years.

Enormous damage was done to the medieval, Renaissance and Baroque fabric of the historic, unreformed city, when numerous monasteries, palaces, villas and gardens vanished under bricks and mortar. In the process, the remains of ancient Rome were stumbled on by accident, and dug up unsystematically with no proper record.

How did all this frenzied activity affect the Forum? It may not come as a surprise to find that, following the example of Napoleon and of popes Pius VII and IX, and Pope Leo XII, the new monarchs took advantage of the opportunities for legitimising their rule by restoring ancient Roman monuments, especially those in the Forum. The principal excavations were thus not due to the republicans or the popes, but to the enemies of the popes, King Victor Emmanuel II (reigned 1861–78) and King Umberto I (reigned 1878–1900). In 1875 Victor Emmanuel II founded the Italian School of Archaeology, modelled on the French and German institutes, while in the Forum attention was turned to clearing the central area, after which almost the whole site was levelled. The work was partly prompted by an ambition to reduce unemployment. Three successive phases here were directed by Pietro Rosa from 1871–75, by Rodolfo Lanciani from 1882–4, and by Giacomo Boni from 1898–1925. 'From February to April 1882,' wrote Lanciani, 'more than 10,200 cubic metres of earth were removed and cleared, and 2,800 square metres of ancient ground were uncovered.' He added proudly that, 'For the first time since the fall of the Roman Empire, one could walk along the entire length of the Via Sacra from where it started to the Capitoline.' In 1882, he also removed the two principal roads that cut through the Forum, the Via Bonella and the Via S. Lorenzo/S. Maria Liberatrice. It was he who was responsible for creating as the principal entrance to the Forum the unpleasant ramp that still exists between the Basilica Aemilia and the Temple of Antoninus and Faustina.

Reactions to the changes in Rome were, of course, sharply divided. They were welcomed by David Silvagni, who published a three-volume Protestant attack on Rome in the 1880s. He claimed that,

*There is probably no city in Europe where the influence of the medieval times lingered so long as in Rome. Up to the year 1870, it only needed to pass through its gates to enter upon quite a new world ... But in spite of its artistic effect, and its profane assumption of holiness, this ancient régime was as corrupt as it well could be. The greatest ambitions were hidden under the veil of sanctity; society was rotten to the core.*

The examples of corruption which he cited ranged from the claim that 'the Albano Princes possessed the right to make pins at Urbino, and whoever ventured to import them from elsewhere was punished with fines and floggings,' to the complaint that 'The castration of children was also a monopoly, and belonged to a barber in the Via Papali.'

By contrast, in a book which Augustus Hare dedicated 'To His Dear Mother, the Constant companion of Many Roman Winters', he memorably complained that,

*Twenty-six years of Sardinian rule – 1870–96 – have done more for the destruction of Rome than all the invasions of the Goths and Vandals. If the Government, the Municipality, and, it must be confessed, the Roman aristocracy, had been united together since 1870, with the sole object of annihilating the beauty and interest of Rome, they could not have done it more effectually. The old charm is gone for ever, the whole aspect of the city is changed ... the pagan ruins have been denuded of all that gave them picturesqueness or beauty.*

A key enemy for Hare was the ebullient Rodolfo Lanciani, who was probably not much troubled by the effusions of Hare, whom he might have dismissed as 'a mother's boy'. For long the key figure in the Forum and elsewhere, Lanciani was an engineer, archaeologist, teacher and journalist and the author of an astonishing number of books, including several written in English to catch the Anglo-American market. His over-confidence allowed him unwisely to declare as early as 1897 that the Forum and Palatine 'have been largely, if not completely, excavated since 1879'. One is tempted to see him as something of a mountebank or at least as the Mr Toad of the Roman archaeological world. He was disliked by scholars such as Gregorovius for his support of the post-1871 government of Rome, which permitted indiscriminate building to destroy so much of ancient as well as of medieval and Renaissance Rome.

Lanciani absolved the government in a remarkable passage in which, not mentioning the destruction in his own day, he suggested that the damage done to Roman monuments by the barbarian invaders was 'hardly worth considering when compared with the guilt of others. By "others" I mean the Romans themselves, of the Imperial, Byzantine, Mediaeval and Renaissance periods.' Of course, the government had made possible his extensive excavations in the Forum and elsewhere, so he rewarded his masters by organising a great exhibition in 1911 to celebrate the fiftieth anniversary of Italian unity, an idea developed by Mussolini in his spectacular exhibition of 1937–8, the Mostra Augustea della Romanità.

The greatest achievements of Lanciani were probably his work on the marble plan, the *Forma Urbis Romae*, one of the most iconic symbols of Rome, and his book on the excavations, *Storia degli scavi*. Always committed to bringing archaeology alive, Lanciani took his students each year to see a village of straw huts near Gabii (Castiglione), east of Rome, to demonstrate his belief that primitive settlements in the Forum and Palatine in the eighth century BC 'must have looked like the temporary villages which the peasants of the present day build in the Pontine marshes or in the Agro Romano when they come down from their mountains for the cultivation of the maize-fields.' Also, following his excavation in 1878 of the ancient Roman Via Nova, twenty-three metres wide, which led from the Septizonium on the side of the Palatine Hill to the Baths of Caracalla, he explained that the principal artery of modern Rome, the Via Nazionale, was only two metres wider.

One wonders, in his reference to the damage done in 'the Imperial, Byzantine, Mediaeval and Renaissance periods', what period he had in mind by 'Imperial': can he really have meant to condemn additions to the Forum from the first to the fourth century AD? Since for him the Baroque period had also harmed the Forum, he complained that the church of S. Adriano had damaged the Curia and that the Early Christian church of S. Martina 'was disfigured by Pietro da Cortona'; he was even hostile to the church of SS. Cosmas and Damian. Yet he was open enough to point out that 'Pagan temples, like our Renaissance churches, were at the same time places of worship and museums of Fine Arts.' Another resonant aperçu was his claim that, despite their interest in antique art, the popes were indifferent to Christian antiquities from the Renaissance until the time of Pius IX in the mid nineteenth century, a paradox worthy of contemplation.

# 7

---

# FROM MUSSOLINI AND HITLER TO
# HOLES IN THE GROUND

## THE ASSAULT ON THE CHURCHES

Readers of this book will have gathered by now that much of what we are allowed to visit today in the Forum, except for the rarely seen churches, is nineteenth or twentieth century in date, notably the Temple of Vesta, Shrine of Juturna, Rostra, Temple of Divus Julius, and Portico of the Harmonious Gods. In the imaginative re-creation of the Forum, first fictional then physical, Rodolfo Lanciani played, as we have seen, a key role. He has been described as belonging to the old antiquarian school of description rather than analysis.

His successor, Giacomo Boni, who made the second major archaeological contribution to the Forum, was a complete contrast. Trained as an architect and with an interest in geology and construction, he wielded not a pen but a pickaxe, emerging from academic libraries to work on site as an active archaeologist. He believed in uncovering a site to take it back to its origins in a systematic exposure of different layers, in a process known as 'stratigraphic excavation'. He began this in the Forum for the first time in 1898, showing in due course that at certain points there were more than two dozen archaeological strata underneath each other.

A Venetian, he was confident to dig below the water table in the Forum.

Boni's methods, or his luck, produced his spectacular discovery in June 1899 of the Black Stone, at the east side of the Arch of Septimius Severus. This nearly square slab of dark marble, actually three by four metres, was perhaps the *lapis niger* of ancient authors for whom, according to Late Republican tradition, it marked the location of the tomb of Romulus, founder of Rome, or of his 'ascension' into heaven; or it marked the site of the tomb of the shepherd who fostered him, or of Hostilius, grand-father of the third king of Rome. Digging below this in the hope of discovering the tomb itself, Boni found a stela inscribed in early Latin which read in part, 'Whoever violates this sacred place shall be destined for the infernal gods.' He was undeterred by this alarming threat, which seems to have been a prohibition of the sixth century BC, connected with sanctuaries of Vulcan, god of fire. Inspired by the hope of finding the archaic origins of the Forum, he excavated in 1902–5 a necropolis, or archaic cemetery, on the south side of the Temple of Antoninus and Faustina, where burials ranged from the ninth to the early sixth centuries BC. Boni filled in the graves with plots of grass, circular for cremations, oblong for inhumation. He went on in 1911–25 to uncover the bases of huts of the same period below the Flavian Palace on the Palatine.

Boni shared Lanciani's dislike of all post-antique additions to the Forum, notably the churches. Archaeology thus collided with religion in 1900 when Boni broke into the façade of the church of S. Adriano, which incorporated the Curia, the Senate House. Protesting from the windows above as soon as he climbed in, Spanish monks subsequently complained to the Spanish Ambassador, and the newly created aperture was closed and exploration of the Curia suspended for several years. Boni was accompanied on this illicit adventure by his friend the improbably named Welbore St Clair Baddeley, a rather self-satisfied amateur archaeologist who did much through articles and lectures to promote the achievement of both Lanciani and Boni.

Baddeley recorded that a monk who had heard him lecture on the Basilica Aemilia complained to him that 'he knew not only that he was an out and out Pagan, but that he made others so, and so "spread the poison everywhere by means of a vain enthusiasm. You'll want S. Lorenzo in Miranda next, or S. Maria Liberatrice!"' This was an accurate prophecy, for though S. Lorenzo miraculously escaped destruction, Boni blew up with dynamite the handsome church of S. Maria Liberatrice, its expropriation costing 371,000 lire in compensation. At least the orange trees behind it, cultivated by nuns, were removed to the Palatine where Boni lived. From 1900 the pleasing row of old houses which ran west towards the Curia from the Temple of Antoninus and Faustina was demolished in the hope of revealing something of the Basilica Aemilia. However, the resulting site is a barren mess in which there is virtually nothing to see.

The English, who still took a close interest in what was being done in the Forum, were familiar with the names of both Lanciani and Boni. Baddeley took Rudyard Kipling to the Forum in 1909 to introduce him to Boni, while Lanciani showed Queen Mary round the Forum on her state visit in 1923 with George V, who made Lanciani a Knight Commander of the Royal Victorian Order in the following year. Boni was accorded an obituary in *The Times* in 1925, which supported the view that had grown up among the English that he had learnt from the critic John Ruskin the importance of conserving what is found, even if it is decayed. Ruskin and his disciples passionately opposed restoration on the grounds that it destroyed the precious touch supposedly left by the hands of the original craftsmen. Such a view was, we have seen, hardly shared by Boni, while the claim in his obituary that he chose 'to heal the scars of excavation by the help of nature' exaggerates what was simply the planting of appropriate plants and flowers. Boni's careful stratigraphic approach as an archaeologist was forgotten by his immediate successors and was not revived until the phase of excavations that began in the 1960s and continues to the present day.

The continuing interest in ancient Rome of German, British and American scholars was institutionalised in academic yet socially congenial bodies that still flourish today. These include the Bibliotheca Hertziana, the British School and the American Academy, all with research libraries, students and visiting scholars. The Assistant Director and Librarian of the British School from 1909 was the redoubtable Eugénie Sellers (Mrs Arthur Strong), who lived in Rome for thirty-four years. Her writings were important for no longer seeing Roman art as an imitative appendix to Greek and Hellenistic culture, a judgement which echoed Winckelmann, but was valid in its own right. No less significantly, she rehabilitated the Baroque, till then generally despised, as a worthy successor to pure classicism. Her circle included Sir Rennell Rodd, British Ambassador from 1908, and Rodd's private secretary, Lord Berners, a wealthy aesthete and early modern composer who was a friend of Stravinsky, Diaghilev and the Sitwells. These he entertained in his two Roman residences, notably a delectable house in Via Foro Romano, running along the south side of the Forum behind the Basilica Julia. Its large drawing room had a balcony commanding a fine view of the Forum, and from it friends such as Rex Whistler, Edward James, Diana Mosley, Penelope Betjeman and the exiled Earl Beauchamp (the inspiration for Lord Marchmain in Evelyn Waugh's novel *Brideshead Revisited*), could observe everything going on.

The British Government rather absurdly sent Lady Diana Cooper on a mission to Rome to inform those in power how strongly England opposed Italian aggression in Abyssinia. Lord Berners' house was a natural setting for a diplomatic lunch, at which Lady Diana had a discussion with several close friends of Count Galeazzo Ciano, the Italian foreign minister and son-in-law of Mussolini. With a touch of realism she later asked, 'What hope had I of harnessing Italy from beneath the hospitable roof of 3, Foro Romano?'

## MUSSOLINI

Benito Mussolini attempted to revive an idea of Rome that had served varied political ambitions since the Middle Ages. After the First World War, he founded the Fascio del Combattimento, a militaristic nationalist group that hoped to re-create the ancient grandeur of Rome. It adopted as its symbol the *fasces*, the bundles of rods carried in ancient times by the lictors attending magistrates, whose power to punish they symbolised. On 28 October 1922 Mussolini marched on Rome and established Year I of the Fascist state, obtaining full power of government from King Victor Emmanuel III and the parliament. If Hare had known what Mussolini was going to do to Rome, twenty years after his death, he might have regarded as comparatively trifling the changes that he had so much lamented. To paraphrase Hare's words, Mussolini might almost be seen as having a *sole* object of annihilating the beauty and interest of Rome, for he declared in 1925 that his aim in creating a new Rome was to 'liberate the trunk of the great oak from everything which still smothers it. Open up spaces … Everything which has grown up in the centuries of decadence must be swept away.'

Enormously destructive changes were made to the character of the Forum from 1928, when Mussolini drove along its northern side an immense urban highway, the Via dell'Impero, which he inaugurated on 20 October 1932. This was part of the romantic and not ignoble ambition that, 'five years from now', as Mussolini declared on 31 December 1925, 'Rome must appear in all its splendour: immense, ordered, and powerful as it was at the time of the first empire, that of Augustus.' The accompanying revival of classical studies, Roman history and Latin, can be seen as beneficial; less so the establishment of the Italian Empire by Mussolini on 9 May 1936. Giulio Quirino Giglioli, chief archaeologist of the regime, used his research to argue that the historical and national aims of Fascism were part of a continuous trajectory of Roman history. Giacomo Boni had already stressed the continuity of Roman history by re-enacting in the Forum on 1 March 1922 the solemn ceremony to commemorate the *Natalis Martis*, the birthday of Mars, father of Romulus.

Mussolini explained that the new road along the edge of the Forum, running from the Colosseum to the Palazzo Venezia, was intended 'for great military parades'. It was in the Palazzo Venezia that he had established himself in

September 1929, a palace which, though grandiose enough to most eyes, had been considered by Napoleon, as we have seen, to be fit only to serve as the administrative centre of his proposed imperial palace. Mussolini named his new highway Via dell'Impero (Empire Street), even before the declaration of the Empire in 1936. It was renamed Via dei Fori Imperiali in September 1944, which is ironic, since it obliterated over 84 per cent of the recently excavated forums of Nerva and Trajan. To create it, an area of 40,000 square metres of one of the most historic parts of medieval and Renaissance Rome was destroyed, including five churches and many houses, of which it is now difficult even to find photographs.

On to the walls of the Basilica of Maxentius, adjacent to the Via dell'Impero, Mussolini fastened five large marble maps recording the progressive conquests by Rome from the ancient world onwards. The first four are still in situ, but the fifth, intended to show the possessions of the new Italian empire, is lying in storage in a courtyard at the Museo della Civiltà Romana. Also on the Via dell'Impero Mussolini intended to build the Palazzo Littorio (palace of the lictors), headquarters of the Italian Fascist party, for which a competition was held in 1933. It would be 'modern', that is, not a stylistic copy of anything Roman, but was to have what was called the 'superior and audacious, cool and rationalist character' of the favourite monuments in Rome of the Modernists: the newly stripped Curia in the Forum, the Basilica of Maxentius, and the Colosseum. It was eventually built in 1934–5 on the slopes of Monte Mario on the north-west edge of Rome as part of the Foro Mussolini (now Italico), laid out by Enrico del Debbio as a monumentally planned new area with axial vistas, which is still impressive.

Great streets, axially aligned on monuments, were an aspect of the classical principles of ancient Roman city planning deployed throughout the Roman Empire yet not till now applied to Rome itself. The Forum, in particular, had already become a kind of museum in the ancient world, venerated for the associations of its ancient buildings. However, Napoleon and Mussolini aimed to isolate monuments such as the Mausoleum of Augustus, the Pantheon, and even the Trevi Fountain, and make them intimidating objects in the middle of large squares. Mussolini told his followers, 'you will also free the majestic temples of Christian Rome ... the 1,000-year-old monuments of our history must stand out in isolation as giants,' showing how his reign venerated Classical monuments, the Christian ones, as well as those of modern Fascism.

For the 'liberation' of the Mausoleum of Augustus, the first Roman emperor, Mussolini created a graceless new Piazza Augusto Imperatore in 1934–7, demolishing in the process 27,000 square metres of the city, including eight streets and 120 houses. Further demolition on a vast scale was required for the giant and rather featureless Via della Conciliazione, laid out in 1937 to open up an unnecessary vista of St Peter's from the Tiber. Both this road and the Via dell'Impero were based on projects conceived by Napoleon.

After the excavations of 1874 at the Temple of Venus and Roma, which went down to and exposed the ancient street level, nothing was done until the remains were imaginatively tidied up under Mussolini in 1934–5. The plan of the temple was now partially re-created as an attractive garden with shrubs and flowers, and trees for columns. The double colonnades of grey granite columns that originally lined the north and south sides of the vast platform on which the temple sat were also partially reconstructed. They can be seen by the car park on the north of S. Francesca Romana, and some also line a section of the Via Sacra leading up to the Arch of Titus. Regrettably, the temple and garden are not readily accessible to the public.

The night-time illumination of the Forum to mark the birth of a son to Napoleon as a symbol of the hoped-for continuity of his regime was recalled by Mussolini's imperial 'theme-park', incorporating ancient monuments between the Forum and the Aventine Hill. This culminated in Fascist exhibitions of national life and achievement, which were held between 1937 and 1939 in the Circus Maximus. Enhanced with monumental promenades, marble columns, fountains and triumphal passage ways, these displays were intended to re-create or bring to life the crumbling remains of the Forum. The programme required floodlights to illuminate 'the archaeological promenades, the Baths of Caracalla, the Palatine and the Aventine'. Film, another modern medium, was also deployed to bring antiquity into the modern world. At the Venice Film Festival of 1937, the Mussolini prize was awarded to a film called *Scipione l'Africano*, in which Scipio, who destroyed Carthage and was hailed by Cicero as the greatest of the Romans, makes a speech to a crowd in the Forum in which he pre-echoes the manner and rhetoric of Mussolini.

## HITLER

The use of visual spectacle to illuminate the magical transforming powers of an absolute ruler, linked Napoleon,

Übersicht:

1. Porta S. Paolo
2. Cestius-Pyramide
3. Aventin
4. Serviusmauer
5. S. Balbina
6. Caracalla-Thermen
7. Obelisk von Axum
8. La Vignola
9. S. Gregorio Magno
10. SS. Giovanni e Paolo
11. Palatin
12. Tempel der Venus u. Roma
13. Konstantinsbogen
14. Colosseum
15. Torre dei Conti di Segni
16. Augustus-Forum
17. Trajans-Forum
18. Trajans-Säule
19. Forum Romanum
20. National-Denkmal
21. Cäsar-Forum
22. Palazzo Venezia
23. Quirinal-Palast

Rom

Die
Einzugsstraße des
Führers

Ankunfts-Bahnhof.

36. *Map of Hitler's journey through Rome in 1938.* On the first day of his state visit, Hitler travelled from the railway station near the Pyramid of Caius Cestius (no. 2), via the Forum (no. 19), to Mussolini's base at the Palazzo Venezia (no. 22), and finally to King Victor Emanuel III at the Quirinal Palace (no. 23).

Mussolini and Hitler, another dictator who attempted to re-create for his own purposes the architectural might of the Roman Empire. Albert Speer had devised for him a wondrous cathedral of light for the rally of 1934 on the Zeppelin Field at Nuremberg, while Hitler was attracted by the idea that the most important buildings in ancient Rome were not the villas and palaces of individuals, or even commercial premises, but the public buildings and temples of the state, representing the entire people.

For Hitler's triumphant visit to Rome in 1938, an official illustrated map was published with German captions, showing the route (devised by Mussolini) for his arrival on the night of 3 May at the rebuilt Ostia railway station near the Pyramid of Caius Cestius (fig. 36). The principal monuments Hitler passed in his horse-drawn carriage were lit by 45,000 sets of electric lamps, linked by 100 miles of cabling, creating 'a symphony of lights' of different colours and substances. The route took him to the Colosseum and the Forum, along Mussolini's new Via dell'Impero, then past the Monument to Victor Emmanuel II (which takes on a Germanic flavour in its labelling on this map as the National-Denkmal), past Mussolini's seat of power at the Palazzo Venezia, and finally to the Quirinal Palace, where he was to stay with the King until 9 May.

The stress on architecture, especially antique architecture, on a state visit to seal the Axis alliance is surely remarkable. It was little more than a year later that Hitler's invasion of Poland ignited the Second World War. Nonetheless, he chose to pay two lengthy visits to Mussolini's great exhibition of 'Roman-ness', the Mostra Augustea della Romanità in the Palazzo delle Esposizioni in the via Nazionale, which had been inaugurated on 23 September 1937, the 2,000th anniversary of the first emperor's birth. The Forum of Augustus had just been excavated, casually and without measurements or records being taken, while the Mostra contained no ancient artefacts but was an essentially modern display of photomontages and over 300 models of famous monuments from all over the old Roman Empire. The most spectacular of these was the great model of Rome as it was at the beginning of the fourth century, with a brilliant re-creation of the Forum at its heart. The model was largely inspired by Lanciani's *Forma Urbis Romae*, the plans of Rome that he had published in 1893.

Ranuccio Bianchi Bandinelli, the archaeologist who, because he spoke German, was chosen to conduct Hitler round the ruins, was a Marxist, which was ironic in view of the great battle against Bolshevism that Hitler was soon to launch. Hitler spent several hours in the Colosseum, meditating on the plans of the new Congress Hall at Nuremberg which had been inspired by it. He had already decided that public buildings in the Reich should no longer be of steel girders and reinforced concrete but of the marble, stone and brick that he admired in the ruins of the Forum. He wanted to 'build a bridge of tradition with which to communicate heroic aspirations to future generations'. This was in accordance with Speer's *Theorie von Ruinenwert* (*Theory of Ruin Value*) in which, as Speer put it, 'By using special materials and by applying certain principles of statics, we should be able to build structures which even in a state of decay, after hundreds … or thousands of years would more or less resemble Roman models.'

Speer had a romantic drawing prepared of what his

reviewing stand at the Zeppelin Field at Nuremberg 'would look like after generations of neglect, overgrown with ivy, its columns fallen, the walls crumbling here and there'. Though members of his entourage were alarmed at this, Hitler was persuaded by Speer's arguments. Indeed, in the Cabinet Room at Speer's new Chancellery in Berlin of 1938–9, Hitler chose to hang two paintings of the ruins in the Forum by Hubert Robert. This celebrated master of ruin-painting had lived for eleven years from 1754 in Rome, where he was influenced by the vision of Piranesi.

In 2006 the discovery was announced of a collection of Speer's drawings and papers in Moscow, which showed for the first time that Hitler commissioned him to re-create in Berlin a version of St Peter's Square in Rome, but with a statue of Mussolini, not an Egyptian obelisk, in the centre. Hitler saw the model for this project as well as several castings of the statue. But his dreams were short-lived. In 1944, just six years after Hitler's visit to the Forum, soldiers of the Allied Forces entrusted with the capture of Rome were issued with guidebooks 'to ensure that the most important sites remained undamaged, where possible – and that visitors, too, should recognise the monuments of their own cultural heritage.'

## THE MYTH OF ROME FROM 1950 TO THE PRESENT DAY

It was intended that the contents of the Mostra Augustea della Romanità would be re-used in 1942 in the Universal Exposition in Rome (Espozione Universale di Roma, known as EUR) to celebrate the conquest of Ethiopia and the twentieth anniversary of the Fascist regime. Work began in 1938 on monumental buildings for this purpose, filling a large area in southern Rome, but it ceased during the Second World War. However, work on realising Mussolini's vision was renewed in 1952, one part of the project, the Museo della Civiltà Romana (Museum of Roman Civilisation) being opened in 1955. It contains materials from Lanciani's exhibition of 1911 and the large Mostra of 1937, including the great model.

Back in the Forum, excavation from the 1950s onwards has followed the two principal innovations of Boni: the stratigraphic technique and the interest in the earliest archaic period. This contrasted with the majority of the excavations under Mussolini, which tended to concentrate, for political reasons, on the imperial period. One of the most disastrous of the new traffic highways created by Mussolini in the heart of Rome was, and remains, the Via del Teatro di Marcello, skirting the western base of the Capitoline Hill. Opened in 1933, this led to the scheduling for government offices in 1937 of an adjacent area by the church of S. Omobono de' Sartori in the Vico Jugario.

Approached by a flight of steps, S. Omobono has a modest Renaissance façade of the 1570s, like that of the demolished S. Maria Liberatrice only without the volutes. Excavations to test the soil for foundations revealed fragments of a temple and part of its sixth century BC podium. Further exploration in 1959–64 and 1986 revealed a characteristically Roman palimpsest, including evidence of habitation as early as the Bronze Age (fourteenth to thirteenth centuries BC), of Iron Age huts of the seventh century BC, and of the building in 1482 of the church later dedicated to S. Omobono. Though significant for revealing the presence of Etruscans in the seventh and eighth centuries BC, as well as of fragments of imported Greek pottery of the eighth century, the remains, partly visible behind the inevitable railings, are uninviting.

Excavation in the Forum became increasingly international, the Swede Einar Gjerstad working there from the 1950s into the 1970s, uncovering twenty-nine layers which suggested that, so far from being founded in 753 BC, as used to be believed, Rome was the result of a gradual period of settlement over several centuries. The earliest building of importance Gjerstad found was suggested by paving near the Via Sacra that he dated to the early sixth century BC. However, Andrea Carandini, Professor of Archaeology at Rome University, who has been excavating in the Forum since 1985, made an important discovery in 1987, several metres lower than the excavations of either Boni or Gjerstad. Below Vespasian's markets facing the Basilica of Maxentius, he uncovered the so-called 'Wall of Romulus'. Dated to *c.* 730–720 BC, this is represented merely by a foundation trench filled with rough lumps of tufa and earth. It is presumed that the wall rising from it would have been a palisade of timber and clay defining the sacred space of the city and conforming very roughly with the old story of the foundation of Rome in 753 BC. After various rebuilding phases, it seems that the first actual stone wall in *opus quadratum* went up in *c.* 600 BC. It was demolished in *c.* 530 BC to make way for stone-built aristocratic houses on the slope behind it, which even at this early date incorporated the Roman atrium into their plan. These excavations have been partly covered over.

More extensive excavations, begun immediately behind the Senate House and Basilica Aemilia in 1996, are still in progress. They shed light for scholars on the relation of the

Forum to the adjacent forums of Caesar, Augustus, Nerva and Trajan. However, since this was already a dense and confusing tangle in antiquity, made worse by the driving through it of the Via dei Fori Imperiali, the excavations complicate rather than clarify the area for the visitor.

In 1989, a group led by Leonardo Benevolo, an architectural historian and specialist in urban planning, reacted against the increasingly arid results of the archaeologists' work and proposed the creation of a vast archaeological park with trees and walkways, extending through central Rome from the forums to the Baths of Caracalla. It recalled the Napoleonic 'Jardin du Capitol', but it had little chance of being executed, because Rome is not just a museum town but the working capital city of a large European state (a combination which makes it a more stimulating place to visit than Florence, say). The scheme would have also removed entirely the Via dei Fori Imperiali, to which the city planners have a great attachment, even though the Communists, still a presence in Italy, would like to see it go as a symbol of Fascism, the battle against which they try to keep alive.

Professor Carandini believes that the traces found on the Palatine of eighth-century Iron Age huts from the time of Romulus have led us falsely to believe that the Rome of Romulus was a simple community of shepherds and farmers living in wattle and daub huts. Near the House of the Vestals, he has found a paved floor suggesting an open space for public gatherings and an oval structure where the Virgins kept three eternal flames burning. Thus, he says, a fully fledged city was in operation as early as the mid eighth century, with a king and religious rites. If so, Numa Pompilius in the seventh century was not the first king to organise a state religion, and it was not under the Etruscan kings that the Forum was drained and paved but under Romulus.

Indeed, as we noted in Chapter 1, Professor Carandini discovered holes in the floor of the Forum in 2005 which he took to be footings for supports in the palace of Romulus. It seems quite extraordinary that a romantic nineteenth-century obsession with finding the 'palace' of the mythical Romulus persists, rather as though modern British archaeologists should seek to uncover the palace of Merlin. An element of fantasy lay behind an article in *The Times* in August 2005 which described Carandini's discovery as 'a huge and impressive royal palace of the eighth century BC in the Forum, next to the Temple of the Vestal Virgins'. Supposedly 'entered through a monumental colonnaded porch, it covered 345 square metres with an open courtyard in the centre of the complex'. It was further claimed that, though rebuilt several times after fires, 'it survived until the collapse of the Roman Empire in the fifth century AD', its remains subsequently being re-used in Renaissance buildings. The article was illustrated with a photograph of the eight columns of the Temple of Saturn, set up in their present form in AD 360–80, but unidentified in the caption so as to suggest they either were, or resembled, the archaic palace.

By chance, this romantic vision of the halls of an eighth-century palace, was contradicted in the same year in a spectacular BBC television epic of ancient Rome, which stressed what the director felt, probably correctly, were the filth, squalor and heat of the city. The actors and wardrobe designers were all sent to live for a time in Calcutta to gain appropriate experience, while scenes of sex of all kinds were advertised as the principal attraction of the eleven-part film. The Forum was re-created in fibreglass, six miles from Rome in the Cinecittà studios, but the Temple of Jupiter Capitolinus was moved down to it from its home on the Capitoline Hill.

The early days of 2006 saw the announcement of the discovery in the Forum of a tomb which Alessandro Delfino, the archaeologist leading the excavation, identified as that of a clan chief of the late ninth century BC. Containing a funerary urn, ceramics and vases, this was claimed by Professor Eugenio La Rocca, Superintendent of Archaeology in Rome, as evidence of a 3,000-year-old necropolis. It was thus purported to show that there had been organised habitation in Rome between the end of the Bronze Age and the beginning of the Iron Age. La Rocca went on to envisage a collection of villages close to the Tiber at least a century before the legendary foundation of Rome by Romulus and Remus. This was quite a lot to build on the remains of a single tomb. Andrea Carandini observed that, even if Delfino's suppositions were correct, Romulus and Remus were still the founders of Rome in the sense that they had created the first cohesive walled city.

### THE DESTRUCTION OF ROME?

A brilliant little book by Claude Moatti, *The Search for Ancient Rome* (1993), ends with a chilling hint of the fate some archaeologists might have in mind for Rome: nothing less than its destruction. She states that, 'So much remains to be excavated that it is truly impossible to estimate its riches. We still know very little, for example about the Campus Martius.' This is, of course, the very heart of Rome, rich with churches, piazzas and palaces, like the Piazza Navona, S. Maria Sopra

Minerva and the Palazzo Farnese, yet all this could be dismissed by some, as Dr Moatti points out, as merely 'the piling up of material over the centuries'. Proponents of this view would regret that in this part of Rome, 'The Circus of Flaminius, the three temples of Jupiter, Juno, and Hercules, and the Theatre of Bacchus are all still hidden.' Moatti points out that,

> We know quite precisely that, for example, we would find the ruins of the Temple of Jupiter beneath the church of Santa Maria in Campitelli. The piling up of material over the centuries has been continuous in that district of the city, and only the Portico of Octavia reflects some of its former splendour. One would have to dig very deeply indeed.

It would be alarming if a new generation of archaeologists were to follow twentieth-century precedent by 'digging deeply' and destroying Baroque monuments in order to expose ruined fragments of Roman buildings and foundations. Surely a masterpiece like Rainaldi's columnar façade of S. Maria in Campitelli of the 1660s is more able than these fragments to convey through its present splendour the 'former splendour' of ancient Rome. Moreover, recent excavations round the Portico of Octavia, exposing the usual scraps of foundation walls, now protected by metal walkways, have wrecked a beautiful area of Rome where the Portico suggested the splendour of antiquity far better when it was embedded in later and more modest vernacular buildings and streets.

Indeed, some may agree with Sigmund Freud that when seeing the Palazzo Caffarelli on the Capitoline Hill, built in 1584 on part of the podium of the vanished Temple of Jupiter

Capitolinus, we can simultaneously experience both palace and temple. In his book *Civilisation and its Discontents*, Freud presented the eternal image of Rome as the perfect analogy to the human mind, where all things are preserved in the form of memory, arguing that,

> *In the place occupied by the Palazzo Caffarelli would once more stand – without the palace having to be removed – the Temple of Jupiter Capitolinus; and this, not only in its latest shape, as the Romans of the Empire saw it, but also in its earliest one, when it still showed Etruscan forms and was ornamented with terracotta antefixes. Where the Coliseum now stands we would at the same time admire Nero's vanished Goldenhouse.*

Let us hope that no one will ever again agree with Nikolaus Pevsner's astonishing claim, in his influential book *Outline of European Architecture* (1943), that 'The Greek temple, most readers probably agree, and the Roman forum, belong to the civilisation of Antiquity, not to what we usually mean when we speak of European civilisation.' This was a product of his belief that western architecture culminated in the Modern Movement of the early twentieth century and that what did not contribute to the 'progress' which led to this could be left out of the story.

THE FUTURE OF ROME?

The work of archaeologists has naturally been used extensively in the course of writing this book where, at the start, the recent revival of interest in the history of the classical world was emphasised. We can end by pointing to the existence of a parallel revival in the work of current architects on both sides of the Atlantic who, like Freud in the passage just quoted, have returned to an architecture of memory through their understanding and practice of the classical language of architecture. The public buildings and temples in the Forum and elsewhere in Rome had been the model for the majority of public buildings erected between the Renaissance and the 1930s. Among the many spectacular examples from the 1930s are the National Archives and the Jefferson Memorial in Washington, DC, by John Russell Pope (1874–1937), whose designs show study of monuments such as the Pantheon, Hadrian's Temple of Venus and Roma and Augustus' Temple of Mars Ultor.

When building resumed after the Second World War, a Modernist language that eschewed all historical resonance became a near-universal norm for about forty years. However, in the 1980s a mood of pluralism set in, which, by the turn of the century, had led to the growth of full-blooded classicists, especially in Britain and the United States of America. Today, the offices of architects such as Quinlan and Francis Terry, John Simpson, Demetri Porphyrios, Robert Adam, Hugh Petter, Craig Hamilton, Robert Stern, Liam O'Connor, Léon Krier, Allan Greenberg and Thomas Gordon Smith contain much-thumbed copies of the works of Vitruvius and of architects such as Palladio. As a result, measured drawings of the orders of the temples and public buildings in the Forum are once again tools in the process of design, while there are also new commentaries on Vitruvius. One of these was published in 1999 by Ingrid Rowland and Thomas Noble Howe, and one in 2003 by the architect, Thomas Gordon Smith, with illustrations of the five of the ten books comprising Vitruvius' treatise which Smith considers to be of most relevance to a modern practising architect. Measured drawings of the orders of the temples and public buildings in the Forum are once again tools in the process of design. The unfolding narrative of the long history of the Roman Forum has thus reached a stimulating new chapter, though certainly not the last. As Palladio predicted, 'The Forum offers the pilgrim not the spectacle of ancient glory but rather the possibility of re-creating it.'

# MAKING A VISIT

The Forum is open daily from 8.30 a.m. to one hour before sunset (closed 1 January, 25 December). Opening hours are correct at the time of writing but may be subject to change. Admission is by ticket, currently 12 euros, which also gives access to the Palatine and the Colosseum. There are two public entrances to the Forum, of which the more widely used, but entirely modern and unattractive, is the northern one from Mussolini's Via dei Fori Imperiali. The other is from the east, in the Via di San Gregorio, which is also convenient for the Palatine. There are also two exits, one at the east end from near the Arch of Titus, and one on the north side at the west end in the Via di S. Pietro in Carcere. The nearest subway station is Colosseo, on Line B. Tram no. 3 goes to the Colosseum.

The inadequate Forum shop at the entrance from the Via dei Fori Imperiali has a far from comprehensive collection of books and postcards. No substantial refreshments are on sale in the Forum, and the nearby restaurants are no more than adequate. The Hotel Forum in the quiet Via di Tor de' Conti just off the Via dei Fori Imperiale, has a roof terrace with a splendid view of the Forum looking south.

**Antiquarium Forense** (the Forum Museum), an important collection of sculpture and architectural fragments from the Forum. Entrance is from the Forum by the side of S. Francesca Romana at no. 53 Piazza S. Maria Nova. Open daily from 8.30 a.m. to one hour before sunset.

**Temple of Venus and Roma**, visible from the eastern entrance to the Forum by the Arch of Titus. Open to the public only 'on request' (to the Soprintendenza Archeologica, tel. 06–6998417).

**S. Maria Antiqua** and **Shrine of Forty Martyrs**. Near the centre of the Forum on the south side. Currently closed for restoration.

**Farnese Gardens**, terraces and pavilions, commanding excellent views of the Forum and Basilica of Maxentius. Entrance and ticket kiosk near the Arch of Titus. Open daily 8.30 a.m.–7 p.m. (4 p.m. in winter). From this point one can walk, free of charge, up the Via di San Bonaventura, a tree-lined pathway, to two small churches:

**S. Sebastiano al Palatino**, and **S. Bonaventura**, further on to the left, both normally open 9 a.m.–12 noon and 3–6 p.m., Monday to Saturday.

Note: many of the churches listed here seem devoted principally to wedding services and are thus often closed to the public.

**S. Lorenzo de' Speziali in Miranda,** now **Nobile Collegio Chimico Farmaceutico** (in the Temple of Antoninus and Faustina). Open Thursday 10 a.m.–12 noon, ring bell at Via in Miranda 10, by the entrance to the Forum from the Via dei Fori Imperiali.

**SS. Cosmas and Damian** and convent; view into 'Temple of Romulus'. Entrance in the Via dei Fori Imperiali by the entrance to the Forum. Open daily 9 a.m.–1 p.m. and 4–7 p.m.

**S. Francesca Romana** (or Sta Maria Nuova). Entrance from the Piazza di Sta Francesca Romana, approached from the Via dei Fori Imperiali, near the Colosseum. Open daily 9.30 a.m.–12 noon and 4–7 p.m.

**Tabularium museum.** Entrance from the Palazzo dei Musei Capitolini on the Capitoline Hill. Open daily, 9 a.m.–8 p.m.

**S. Giuseppe dei Falegnami** in the Clivus Argentarius, approached from the Via di San Pietro in Carcere. Usually open except when weddings are happening. Below the portico of this church is the entrance to the **Mamertine Prison**. Open daily, 9 a.m.–7 p.m.

**SS. Luca e Martina.** Entrance in the Via della Curia. Open daily 9 a.m. to one hour before sunset. Closed 1 January, 1 May and 25 December.

**Museo della Civiltà Romana** (Museum of Roman Civilisation), Piazza Agnelli 10, EUR quarter (Espozione Universale di Roma), on southern edge of Rome. Well worth visiting for the fabulous model of the City of Rome made for Mussolini's Mostra Augustea della Romanità of 1937. The museum also contains reproductions of objects from the Forum. Open daily, 9 a.m.–2 p.m, Sundays 9 a.m.–1.30 p.m. Closed Mondays and 1 January, 1 May and 25 December.

## NOT TO BE MISSED IN THE CHURCHES

**SS. Cosmas and Damian** Carved gilt wood ceiling of 1632 by Luigi Arigucci, with central fresco by Marco Montagna (*fl.* 1618–40). Three chapels on each side of the nave with paintings by Giovanni Baglione (1571–1644) and Baroque frescoes by Francesco Allegrini, a follower of Pietro da Cortona.

**S. Lorenzo de Speziali** Dramatic altar-piece of *c.* 1647 by Pietro da Cortona, *Martyrdom of St Lawrence*, a little-known work of great brilliance, in which this third-century deacon wears sumptuous Baroque vestments, with yards of fluttering lace dominating the painting.

**S. Francesca Romana** *Apse:* Confessio or shrine built in 1638 over the tomb of S. Francesca in the crypt below. This curved architectural screen of four marble columns shelters a depiction of her with her guardian angel carved in marble in 1866–9 by the sculptor Giosuè Meli. This echoes the gilt-bronze relief of her by Gianlorenzo Bernini (1598–1680) of 1644–9, destroyed in 1798 when French troops damaged the church and screen which were restored in 1816–29. Cosmatesque pavement with mosaics of 1160 of the Virgin and saints including the radiating fan pattern found in ancient Roman mosaics at Pompeii, also featuring in mid twelfth-century mosaics in St Maria in Trastevere in Rome. 'Martyrdom of Six Saints', painted by Giovanni Angelo Canini (c. 1617–66). Over the high altar a twelfth- or thirteenth-century panel painting of the Virgin and Child.

*South transept*: Gothic monument carved in alabaster. Wall monument of 1585 by Pietro Paolo Olivieri to Pope Gregory XI de Beaufort (1370–78), who returned reluctantly from Avignon in 1377.

*Sacristy*: A rare, sixth- or seventh-century icon of the Virgin and Child known as the Madonna Glycophilousa and doubtless brought here from S. Maria Antiqua. A characteristic Roman palimpsest, this giant work was uncovered in 1950 beneath a repainting of the nineteenth century over the painting of the Virgin and Child above the high altar noted above. Painting, attributed to Perino del Vaga, of Cardinal Reginald Pole (1500–1558), Archbishop of Canterbury from 1556 to 1558. Shown conversing with Pope Paul III with Roman ruins in the background. The pope made him a cardinal in 1536 for having written a document condemning the royal supremacy that Henry VIII had assumed over papal authority.

*Crypt*: marble relief by Ercole Ferrata (1610–86) of S. Francesca and her angel.

The interior of the church was restored by Pope Pius XII in 1952 but is once again in need of cleaning.

**S. Giuseppe dei Falegnami** Frescoes of 1880 in the apse by Angelo Maccaroni and Cesare Mariani. In the former palazzo of the guild or confraternity, adjacent on the right, is an oratory of 1627 that can be approached from the right aisle of the church. It contains an altar by Tiberio Calcagni (1532–65); frescoes of 1631–7 by Marco Tullio Montagna (*fl.* 1618–40); and a painting of the *Virgin with St Joseph and St Joachim* by Pier Leone Ghezzi (1674–1755).

# FURTHER READING

## GENERAL AND INTRODUCTORY

It is stimulating and perhaps surprising to find that in the twenty-first century the art and architecture, history, politics and religion, of the Roman world should still be the subject of passionate exploration by leading scholars on both sides of the Atlantic. The books cited here will confirm this as well as demonstrate that, after centuries of study, there is still much to be discovered about the Forum, a place that has become a centre of lively debate.

The best modern guidebooks to Rome by archaeologists are Amanda Claridge *et al.*, *Rome: An Oxford Archaeological Guide* (Oxford, 1998), and Filippo Coarelli, *Rome and Environs: An Archaeological Guide* (Berkeley and Los Angeles, 2007).

Other reliable academic studies include Coulston and Hazel Dodge, eds., *Ancient Rome: The Archaeology of the Eternal City* (Oxford, 2000); Claude Moatti, *In Search of Ancient Rome* (1989; English translation, London, 1993), a small but well-illustrated and stimulating book; Eva Margareta Steinby, ed., *Lexicon Topographicum Urbis Romae*, (5 vols., Rome, 1993–9), an essential work mainly in Italian but with some chapters in English; Lawrence Richardson, *A New*

*Topographical Dictionary of Ancient Rome* (Baltimore, 1992);
Samuel Ball Platner and Thomas Ashby, *A Topographical Dictionary of Ancient Rome* (Oxford, 1968); Ernest Nash, *A Pictorial Dictionary of Ancient Rome* (2 vols., 2nd edn, London, 1968); Mary Boatwright, *Hadrian and the City of Rome* (Princeton, 1987); Diane Favro, *The Urban Image of Augustan Rome* (Cambridge, 1996); and Catharine Edwards and Greg Woolf (eds.), *Rome the Cosmopolis* (Cambridge, 2003). The many historic plans of the city of Rome are conveniently assembled in Amato Frutaz, *Piante di Roma* (Rome, 1962).

The lengthy entry on ancient Rome in Volume 27 of the *Grove Dictionary of Art* (34 vols., London, 1996), is a rich mine of information. Rome is a city with many guidebooks of a more popular character, beginning with the ever-entertaining Augustus Hare's *Walks in Rome*, first published in 1871 (2 vols., 14th edn, London, 1897). Standard works for the general reader include Henry Vollam Morton, *A Traveller in Rome* (London, 1957); Georgina Masson, *The Companion Guide to Rome* (1965; revised edn by Jim Jepson, Woodbridge, 2000); and Alta Macadam, *Blue Guide to Rome and its Environs* (1974; 6th edn, London and New York, 1998). Especially well informed and varied is John Varriano, *A Literary Companion to Rome* (1991, reprinted London, 2001), while Donald Dudley, *Urbs Roma: A Sourcebook of Classical Texts on the City and its Monuments* (London, 1967), reproduces key ancient texts with new accounts of the buildings described in them, accompanied by illustrations.

On building types and individual buildings in Rome, apart from those in the Forum, the following are helpful: Margaret Scherer, *Marvels of Ancient Rome* (New York and London, 1955), which is well illustrated; James Packer, *The Forum of*

*Trajan: A Study of the Monuments* (4 vols, Berkeley, 1997); and Keith Hopkins and Mary Beard, *The Colosseum* (London, 2005).

The history of Roman architecture is well covered in the following works, of which the first two are by scholars who are also architects interested in what they can still learn from studying these buildings: John Stamper, *The Architecture of Roman Temples: The Republic to the Middle Empire* (Cambridge, 2005), and Mark Wilson Jones, *Principles of Roman Architecture* (New Haven and London, 2000). William MacDonald and John Pinto, *Hadrian's Villa and its Legacy* (New Haven and London, 1995), has a similar aim. Other essential studies are William L. Macdonald, *The Architecture of the Roman Empire 1: An Introductory Study* (1965; rev. edn, New Haven and London, 1982), and *The Architecture of the Roman Empire II:An Urban Appraisal* (New Haven and London, 1986); Margaret Lyttelton, *Baroque Architecture in Classical Antiquity* (London and Ithaca, NY, 1974), the only study of this fascinating subject; Axel Boethius, *Etruscan and Early Roman Architecture* (Harmondsworth, 1978); John B. Ward-Perkins, *Roman Imperial Architecture* (Harmondsworth, 1981); and Gordon Campbell, ed., *The Grove Encyclopedia of Classical Art and Architecture* (2 vols., Oxford, 2007).

On Roman art the following are helpful: Ranuccio Bianchi Bandinelli, *Rome, the Centre of Power: Roman Art to* AD *200* (London, 1970), and *Rome, The Late Empire: Roman Art* AD *200–400* (London, 1971), both well illustrated; Jon J. Pollitt, *The Art of Rome, c. 753* BC–AD *337: Sources and Documents* (1963; reprinted Cambridge, 1991); Donald Strong, *Roman Art* (1976; 2nd edn, Harmondsworth, 1988); Niels Hannestad, *Roman Art and Imperial Policy* (Aarhus, 1986), a thorough account of sculpture; Nancy and Andrew Ramage, *The Cambridge Illustrated History of Roman Art* (Cambridge, 1991); and Otto Brendel, *Prolegomena to the Study of Roman Art* (New Haven and London, 1979), a rare study of different attitudes to Roman art from the eighteenth century onwards.

Finally, since ruins are an essential part of the character of Rome, the following are recommended: Rose Macaulay, *The Pleasure of Ruins* (London, 1953); Carolyn Springer, *The Marble Wilderness: Ruins and Representation in Italian Romanticism, 1775–1750* (Cambridge, 1987); and Christopher Woodward, *In Ruins* (London, 2001).

The quotation on p. 4 from James Joyce is from his *Letters*, Vol. 2, Richard Ellmann, ed. (London, 1966).

## ANCIENT ROMAN TEXTS

Cicero, *In Catilinam* (one of his celebrated orations, delivered in the Forum)

Dio Cassius, *Roman History* (covers the period from the foundation of Rome until AD 229, when the author was aged about eighty. His preference for the Forum of Caesar over the Roman Forum is in Book 4 and his account of the heroism of Marcus Curtius is in Book 1)

Horace, *Odes* (In lyric poems, one of the greatest and most influential of Roman poets ranges from celebrating rural life to glorifying Roman virtues and the rule of Augustus)

Flavius Josephus, *History of the Jewish Wars* (the celebrated account of the triumphal procession of Vespasian through the Forum occurs in Book 7)

Juvenal, *Satires* (a devastating criticism of Roman life, in

striking contrast to the sunny picture painted by his
contemporary, Pliny the Younger)

Livy, *History of Rome* (classic canonisation of Rome from its
foundation to 9 BC)

Pliny (the Elder), *Natural History* (a vast compilation of the
natural world, but including architecture and art history)

Pliny (the Younger), *Letters* (a detailed account of life in
Rome, with a description of his own villas)

Strabo, *Geography* (a lively survey of the physical
characteristics of the Roman world, including the life of
humans, animals and plants, written in Greek around the
end of the first century BC)

Suetonius, *Lives of the Caesars* (the most entertaining of the
contemporary accounts)

Virgil, *Aeneid* (in Book 8, Aeneas is taken to the site of the
future city of Rome)

Vitruvius, *On Architecture* (a key text, the only known
account of its kind to survive from the ancient world)

Translations of these texts and of others cited in this book are
available in the Loeb Classical Library.

CHAPTER I

The many books on the popular subject of life in ancient
Rome include Ludwig Friedlaender, *Roman Life and Manners
under the Early Empire* (4 vols, 1909–13; reprinted London,
1968); Jérôme Carcopino, *Daily Life in Ancient Rome* (1940;
reprinted Harmondsworth, 1981); Andrew William Lintott,
*Violence in Republican Rome* (1968; 2nd edn, Oxford, 1999);
Dacre Balsdon, *Life and Leisure in Ancient Rome* (London,

1969); Florence Dupont, *Daily Life in Ancient Rome* (Oxford, 1993); Kathryn Lomas and Tim Connell, eds., *Urban Society in Roman Italy* (London, 1995); and Mary Beard, *The Roman Triumph* (Harvard, 2007), essential for understanding one of the principal public activities in the Forum. On gladiatorial games in the Forum in the Republican period, see Katherine E. Welch, *The Roman Amphitheatre: From its Origins to the Colosseum* (Cambridge, 2007), pp. 30–68. See also Carlos Machado, 'Building the Past: Monuments and Memory in the Forum Romanum', in William Bowden, Adam Gutteridge, and Carlos Machado eds., *Social and Political Life in Late Antiquity* (Boston, 2006), pp. 157–92.

On Roman history and the Roman world the following are useful studies: Edward Togo Salmon, *The Making of Roman Italy* (Ithaca, 1982); John Boardman *et al.*, *The Oxford History of the Roman World* (Oxford, 1986); Timothy Potter, *Roman Italy* (London, 1987); Nigel Spivey and Simon Stoddart, *Etruscan Italy* (London, 1990), which is important for downgrading the role of Etruscan kings, seeing the growth of Rome and the Etruscan state as equals, borrowing from each other; and Tim J. Cornell, *The Beginnings of Rome: Italy and Rome from the Bronze Age to the Punic Wars (c. 1000–264 BC)* (London and New York, 1995). The definitive study of the role and character of religion in the Roman world is Mary Beard *et al.*, *Religions of Rome* (2 vols., Cambridge, 1998). See also Jocelyn Toynbee, *Death and Burial in the Roman World* (London, 1971).

CHAPTER 2

On Piranesi, see Luigi Ficacci, *Piranesi: The Complete Etchings*

(Cologne, 2000), which reproduces the engravings in his *Le Antichità Romane* and *Vedute di Roma*; and Herschel Levit, *Views of Rome Then and Now: 41 Etchings by Giovanni Battista Piranesi* (New York, 1976), a fascinating and well-informed study which pairs Piranesi's views with modern photographs taken as far as possible from exactly the same point. For a more sophisticated realisation of this idea with the aid of digital photography by Randolph Langenbach in 2003, see 'The Piranesi Project' (www.conservationtech.com). See also Jonathan Scott, *Piranesi* (London, 1975), John Wilton-Ely, *The Mind and Art of G. B. Piranesi* (London, 1978), and Mario Bevilacqua (ed.), *The Rome of Piranesi: The Eighteenth-century City in the Great Vedute* (Rome, 2006). On the Severan Marble Plan, see Gianfilippo Carettoni, *et al.*, *La pianta marmorea di Roma antica* (2 vols., Rome, 1960); and H. Block, 'A New Edition of the Marble Plan of Ancient Rome', *Journal of Roman Studies* 51 (1961).

Of the many monographs on the Forum for a wide audience, the most useful is Michael Grant, *The Roman Forum* (1970; new edn, London, 1974), though now out of print and inevitably lacking information on recent archaeological discoveries. Earlier monographs worth consulting are Rodolfo Lanciani, *The Roman Forum: A Photographical Description of its Monuments* (1910), by a leading archaeologist; Christian Hülsen, *The Roman Forum* (London, 1928); Pirro Marconi, *Le Forum romain* (Paris, 1935); Giuseppe Lugli, *The Roman Forum and the Palatine* (Rome, 1952); Erik Welin, *Studien zur Topographie des Forums Romanum* (Lund, 1953); and Pietro Romanelli, *The Roman Forum* (4th edn, Rome, 1964). *The Roman Forum* (1998; 2nd edn, Rome, 2002), published by the Soprintendenza Archaeologica di Roma, characteristically ignores in text, illustrations and plans the later buildings in and around the Forum.

The contemporary references on pp. 63–4 to the Temple of Castor and Pollux are from Cicero's condemnation of Gaius Verres and from Juvenal's *Satires*. The quotation from Simon Goldhill on the Arch of Titus p. 60 is from *The Temple of Jerusalem* (London, 2004).

CHAPTER 3

Archaeological discoveries since the time of Piranesi are included in two works by Filippo Coarelli: *Il Foro Romano, 1: Periodo Arcaico* (Rome, 1983), and *Il Foro Romano, 2: Periodo Repubblicano e Augusteo* (Rome, 1985), on which see reviews by Nicholas Purcell, 'Rediscovering the Roman Forum', *Journal of Roman Archaeology* 2 (1989), and Peter Wiseman in *Journal of Roman Studies* (1985 and 1986). See also Albert Ammerman, 'On the Origins of the Forum Romanum', *American Journal of Archaeology* 94, no. 4 (1990), and 'The Forum Romanum', *Current Archaeology* 139, (1994); Paul Zanker, *Forum Romanum: Die Neugestgaltung durch Augustus* (Tübingen, 1972), and see review by Richard Brilliant, *Gnomon* 46 (1974); Gianfilippo Carettoni, 'Il Foro Romano', *Studi Romani* II, no. 4 (1963), and 'Excavations and Discoveries in the Forum Romanum and on the Palatine during the last Fifty Years', *Journal of Roman Studies* 50 (1960); E. Gjerstad, *Early Rome* VI (Lund, 1973 etc.), and the review by Arnaldo Momigliano, 'An Interim Report on the Origins of Rome', *Journal of Roman Studies* 53 (1963); Inge Nielsen, 'The Temple of Castor and Pollux on the Forum Romanum ... excavations, 1983–7', *Acta Archaeologica* 59 (1989); and J. W. Rich,

'Augustus's Parthian Honours, the Temple of Mars Ultor and the Arch in the Roman Forum', *Papers of the British School at Rome* 66 (1998).

The references on p. 98 to the opinions of Professor Andrew Wallace-Hadrill on the importance of the Roman imperial court derive from an account of the lecture he delivered at an international conference on *Royal Courts and Capitals* at Sabanci University, Istanbul, 2005.

CHAPTER 4

On the surviving and vanished churches in the Forum from the Early Christian period to the seventeenth century, see two books by Ferruccio Lombardi: *Roma, Chiese, Conventi, Chiostri: Progetto per un Inventario 313–1925* (Rome, 1993), and *Roma, Chiese Scomparse: la Memoria Storica della Città* (Rome, 1996), both useful for their many illustrations though the text is often unreliable. See also Mariano Armellini, *Le Chiese di Roma: Dalle Loro Origini Sino a Secolo XVI* (Rome, 1891); Richard Krautheimer *et al.*, eds., *Corpus Basilicarum Christianarum Romae: The Early Christian Churches of Rome* (5 vols., Rome, 1937–77); Émile Mâle, *The Early Churches of Rome* (London, 1960); Hugo Brandenburg, *Ancient Churches of Rome from the Fourth to the Seventh Century* (Turnhout, 2005); and Maria Hansen, *The Eloquence of Appropriation: Prolegomena to an Understanding of Spolia in Early Christian Rome* (Rome, 2003).

On the religious and historical background, see Arnaldo Momigliano, ed., *The Conflict between Paganism and Christianity in the Fourth Century* (Oxford, 1963); and Hugh Trevor-Roper, *The Rise of Christian Europe* (London, 1965).

On the city of Rome, the following are also essential: Francis Nichols, ed. and trans., *Mirabilia Urbis Romae* (1889; 2nd edn, New York, 1986), the key twelfth-century guide; and John Capgrave, *Ye Solace of Pilgrims: A Description of Rome* c. AD *1450*, ed. Charles A. Mills, (Oxford, 1911). The most important modern study, richly illustrated, is Richard Krautheimer, *Rome: Profile of a City, 312–1308* (1980; rev. edn, Princeton, 2000); but see also Torgil Magnuson, *The Urban Transformation of Medieval Rome, 312–1420* (Stockholm, 2004); Paul Hetherington, *Medieval Rome: A Portrait of the City and its Life* (London, 1994); John R. Curran, *Pagan City and Christian Capital: Rome in the Fourth Century* (Oxford, 2000); and R. Ross Holloway, *Constantine and Rome* (New Haven and London, 2004). Related studies are Michael Greenhalgh, *The Survival of Roman Antiquities in the Middle Ages* (London, 1989); and Bryan Ward-Perkins, *From Classical Antiquity to the Middle Ages: Urban Public Buildings in Northern and Central Italy* AD *300–850* (Oxford, 1984).

On individual churches, see Karl Noehles, *La Chiesa dei SS. Luca e Martina nell'opera di Pietro da Cortona* (Rome, 1970), and John Varriano, 'The 1653 Restoration of S. Adriano in Foro Romano: New Documentation on Martino Longhi the Younger', *Römisches Jahrbuch für Kunstgeschichte* 12 (1970), and 'The Architecture of Martino Longhi the Younger', *Journal of the Society of Architectural Historians* 33 (May 1971). On S. Lorenzo and the 'Temple of Romulus', see Roberta da Mas, 'I Restauri di Orazio Torriano … nell'Area del Foro Romano', *Quaderni dell'Istituto di Storia dell'Architettura* (Rome, 2003), pp. 447–54. See also Antonio Pugliese and Salvatore Rigano, *L'Architettura Barocca a Roma: Studi su Martino Longhi il Giovanni e Pietro da Cortona* (Rome, 1972); and Jörg Mertz, *Pietro da Cortona and Roman Baroque Architecture* (New Haven and London, 2008). The contrasting opinions on the success of the 'restoration' of the Senate House are those of Ward-Perkins (*Roman Imperial Architecture*, 1981), Nash (*Pictorial Dictionary of Ancient Rome*, Vol. 1, 1961), and Dudley (*Urbs Roma*, 1967).

CHAPTER 5

On the romance of ruins in the early Renaissance, see the astonishing illustrated book of 1499 by Francesco Colonna, *Hypnerotomachia Poliphili: The Strife of Love in a Dream* Joscelyn Godwin, trans. (London, 1999). Early attempts at reconstructing Rome and providing guidebooks include Flavio Biondo, *Roma Instaurata* (Rome, 1446), and see D. M. Robathan, 'Flavio Biondo's *Roma Instaurata*', *Medievalia et Humanistica* n.s. (1970); Poggio Bracciolini, *De Varietate Fortunae* (1448), Outi Merisale, ed., (Helsinki, 1993); and Andrea Fulvio, *Antiquitates Urbis* (1527). On Biondo and Bracciolini, see also Frances Muecka, 'Humanism in the Roman Forum', *Papers of the British School at Rome* 71 (2003), pp. 207–33. The central text of Renaissance architecture and theory is Leon Battista Alberti, *On the Art of Building in Ten Books* (1486), Joseph Rykwert, Neil Leach and Robert Tavernor, trans. (Cambridge, Mass., 1988).

The illustrations of buildings in the Forum by Desgodetz, Serlio and Palladio were all hugely influential: Antoine Desgodetz, *Les Edifices Antiques de Rome* (1682); Sebastiano Serlio, *On Architecture*, Books I–VII (1537–75), Vaughan Hart and Peter Hicks, trans. (2 vols, New Haven and London, 1996–2001); and Andrea Palladio, *The Four Books of Architecture*

(1570), Robert Tavernor and Richard Schofield, trans. (Cambridge, Mass., 1997). See also Vaughan Hart and Peter Hicks, eds., *Paper Palaces: The Rise of the Renaissance Architectural Treatise* (New Haven and London, 1998), and *Palladio's Rome* (New Haven and London, 1998).

The following modern studies provide essential background information: Robert Weiss, *The Renaissance Discovery of Classical Antiquity* (1969; 2nd edn, Oxford, 1988); David Thompson, ed., *The Idea of Rome from Antiquity to the Renaissance* (Albuquerque, 1971); Philip Jacks, *The Antiquarian and the Myth of Antiquity: The Origins of Rome in Renaissance Thought* (Cambridge, 1993); and Margaret McGowan, *The Vision of Rome in Late Renaissance France* (New Haven and London, 2000).

On the relation to antiquity of Renaissance architects and garden designers in Rome and the Forum, see Phyllis Lehmann, 'The Basilica Aemilia and S. Biagio at Montepulciano', *Art Bulletin* 64 (March 1982); David Coffin, *Pirro Ligorio: Artist, Architect and Antiquarian* (Pennsylvania State University, 2005); H. Giess, 'Studien zur Farnese-Villa am Palatin', *Römisches Jahrbuch für Kunstgeschichte* 13 (1971); and David Coffin, *Gardens and Gardening in Papal Rome* (Princeton, NJ, 1991).

The writings of visitors to Rome included in this chapter are *The Complete Works of Montaigne*, Donald Frame, trans. (Stanford, 1948); Thomas Nashe, *The Unfortunate Traveller and Other Works* (1594; Harmondsworth, 1984); Francis Osborne, *Advice to a Son* (1658; Ithaca, 1962); H. C. Gent, *The Court of Rome and a Direction for Such as Shall Travell to Rome* (1654); Richard Lassels, *The Voyage of Italy* (1670); *Boswell on the Grand Tour: Italy, Corsica and France, 1765–1766*, Frank

Brady and Frederick Pottle, eds., (London, 1955); Samuel Sharp, *Letters from Italy* (1766); Edward Gibbon, *Autobiography*, M. Reese, ed., (London, 1971), and *Decline and Fall of the Roman Empire* (1776–88; 3 vols., New York, 1946); *The Travel-Diaries of William Beckford of Fonthill*, Guy Chapman, ed., (2 vols., London, 1928); William Beckford, *Dreams, Waking Thoughts and Incidents* (1783), Robert Gemmett, ed., (Rutherford, NJ, 1972); Johann Wolfgang von Goethe, *The Sorrows of Young Werther* (1774), Michael Hulse, trans. (Harmondsworth, 1989), and *Italian Journey* (1786–88), W. H. Auden and Elizabeth Mayor, very freely trans. (London, 1962).

The most useful account of the buildings of seventeenth-century Rome is Anthony Blunt, *Guide to Baroque Rome* (London, 1982), which has a wider coverage than its title suggests. The best study of the whole period is John Varriano, *Italian Baroque and Rococo Architecture* (New York and Oxford, 1986). For the double avenue of elms planted down the centre of the Forum in 1656, see Richard Krautheimer, *The Rome of Alexander VII, 1655–1667* (Princeton, NJ, 1985), Chapter 7, and David Coffin, *Gardens and Gardening in Papal Rome* (Princeton, NJ, 1991), Chapter 11. On the reaction of Claude to the Forum, see I. G. Kennedy, 'Claude and Architecture', *Journal of the Warburg and Courtauld Institutes* 35 (1972); and Helen Langdon, *Claude Lorrain* (Oxford, 1989). Claude's accurate record of the Forum in 1636 is in the Louvre, Paris, no. 311.

The broadest study of the Grand Tour is Ilaria Bignamini and Andrew Wilton, eds., *Grand Tour: The Lure of Italy in the Eighteenth Century* (London, 1996), but see also Catharine Edwards, ed., *Roman Presences: Receptions of Rome in European Culture, 1789–1945* (Cambridge, 1999); Clare Hornsby, ed., *The Impact of Italy: The Grand Tour and Beyond* (London, 2000);

and Frank Salmon, *Building on Ruins: The Rediscovery of Rome and English Architecture* (Aldershot, 2000). For Winckelmann, see David Irwin, ed., *Winckelmann: Writings on Art* (London, 1972); and Alex Potts, *Flesh and the Ideal: Winckelmann and the Origins of Art History* (New Haven and London, 1994).

CHAPTER 6

On the history of archaeological excavation in the Forum in the early nineteenth century, the most thorough account is Ronald Ridley, *The Eagle and the Spade: Archaeology in Rome During the Napoleonic Era* (Cambridge, 1992). Other books on the role of the French include Louis Madelin, *La Rome de Napoléon: La domination française à Rome de 1809 à 1914* (Paris, 1906); Louis Hautecoeur, *Histoire de l'architecture classique en France*, vol. V, *Révolution et Empire 1792–1815* (Paris, 1953); and David Massimiliano, ed., *Ruins of Ancient Rome: The Drawings of French Architects Who Won the Prix de Rome 1786–1924* (Los Angeles, 2002). See also Derek Linstrum, 'The Arch of Titus', *Monumentum: The International Journal of Architectural Conservation*, 25, i (1982).

On some of the figures involved, see Cardinal Nicholas Wiseman, *Recollections of the Last Four Popes and of Rome in their Times* (1858); David Silvagni, *La Corte e la Società Romana nel XVIII Secoli e XIX* (3 vols., Rome, 1883–5), transl. by Fanny McLaughlin as *Rome: Its Princes, Priests and People* (3 vols., London, 1885–7); Owen Chadwick, *The Popes and European Revolution* (London, 1981); John Martin Robinson, *Cardinal Consalvi, 1757–1824* (London, 1987); and Jeffrey Collins, *Papacy and Politics in Eighteenth-century Rome: Pius VI and the Arts* (Cambridge, 2004).

References to the Forum cited in this chapter from the writings of visitors and guides include Lord Byron, *Childe Harold's Pilgrimage* of 1812 (and see John Cam Hobhouse, *Historical Illustrations of the Fourth Canto of Child Harold* (New York, 1818); Percy Bysshe Shelley, *Letters*, vol. 2, F. L. Jones, ed., (Oxford, 1964); *Diaries of Sylvester Douglas*, Francis Bickley, ed., (2 vols., London, 1928); Stendhal (Henri Beyle), *Promenades dans Rome* (1829; Florence, 1958); Thomas Babington Macaulay, 'The Battle of Lake Regillus' in *Lays of Ancient Rome* (1842); *Murray's Hand-Book to Central Italy: Part II: Rome and its Environs* (1843; 4th edn, 1856); and Charles Dickens, *Pictures from Italy* (1846).

Similar sources later in the nineteenth century include *The Roman Journals of Ferdinand Gregorovius, 1852–1874*, Mrs Gustavus W. Hamilton, transl., (London, 1907); George Hillard, *Six Months in Italy* (1853); Nathaniel Hawthorne, *The Marble Faun* (2 vols., 1860), and *Passages from the French and Italian Notebooks* (1871); William Dean Howells, *Italian Journeys* (1867); Walter Pater, *Marius the Epicurean* (1885); and Michael Tyszkiewicz, *Memoirs of an Old Collector* (1898).

Related modern studies include Van Wyck Brooks, *The Dream of Arcadia: American Writers and Artists in Italy 1760–1915* (New York, 1958); John Pemble, *The Mediterranean Passion: Victorians and Edwardians in the South* (Oxford, 1987); Michael Liversidge and Catharine Edwards, *Imagining Rome: British Artists and Rome in the Nineteenth Century* (London, 1996); and David Watkin, *Sir John Soane: Enlightenment Thought and the Royal Academy Lectures* (Cambridge, 1996), which describes the life-long impact on Soane of his stay in Rome in the 1770s and his devotion, as an architect and a teacher, to the monuments in the Forum, notably the

Temple of Castor and Pollux, as a source of inspiration. Count Potocki and his restoration of Pliny's villa are described in Pierre de la Ruffinière du Prey, *The Villas of Pliny from Antiquity to Posterity* (Chicago and London, 1994), a brilliant study of the influence up to the present day of the Younger Pliny's description of his villas. On Carl Fredrik Fredenheim, see Hakan Groth, *Neoclassicism in the North: Swedish Furniture and Interiors 1770–1850* (London, 1990), where Fredenheim's table incorporating fragments of marble from the Forum is illustrated.

For the reliance of Schliemann on Murray's *Handbook to Rome and its Environs*, see Cathy Gere, *The Tomb of Agamemnon: Mycenae and the Search for a Hero* (London, 2006). On Nibby, Lanciani and Boni, the three leading excavators in the Forum in the nineteenth and early twentieth centuries, see Antonio Nibby, *Del Foro Romano, della Via Sacra dell'Anfitreato Flavio* (1819), *Le mura di Roma* (1820), and *Itinerario di Roma e delle sue Vicinanze* (1830); the helpful, though poorly illustrated, monograph on Boni by Eva Tea, *Giacomo Boni nella Vita del Suo Tempo* (2 vols., Milan, 1932); and Domenico Palombi, *Rodolfo Lanciani: l'Archeologia a Roma tra Ottocento e Novecento* (Rome, 2006).

Of Lanciani's huge written output, the most relevant books are *Ancient Rome in the Light of Recent Discoveries* (1888), *Pagan and Christian Rome* (1892; new edn, New York, 1967), *Forma Urbis Romae* (1893–1901; reprinted, Rome, 1990), *The Ruins and Excavations of Ancient Rome: A Companion Book for Students and Travellers* (1897), *The Destruction of Ancient Rome: A Sketch of the History of the Monuments* (1899), *Wanderings through Ancient Roman Churches* (London and Bombay, 1925), and Anthony L. Cubberley, ed., *Notes from Rome by*

*Rodolfo Lanciani* (London, 1988). See also Mary Beard, 'Archaeology and Collecting in Late Nineteenth-Century Rome', in *Ancient Art to Post Impressionism: Masterpieces from the Ny Carlsberg Glyptothek, Copenhagen* (London, 2004).

## CHAPTER 7

For general studies of the modern city, see Italo Insolera, *Roma Moderna: un Secolo di Storia Urbanistica, 1870–1970* (Turin, 1971); and Spiro Kostof, *The Third Rome, 1870–1950: Traffic and Glory* (Berkeley, 1973). On the contribution of Mrs Arthur Strong and her circle, see Gladys Scott Thomson, *Mrs Arthur Strong: A Memoir* (London, 1949); Mary Beard, *The Invention of Jane Harrison* (London, 2000); and Mark Amory, *Lord Berners: The Last Eccentric* (London, 1998).

On the interventions of Mussolini, see Henry Millon and Linda Noechlin, eds., *Art and Architecture in the Service of Politics* (Cambridge, Mass., 1978), Chapter 14; Antonio Cederna, *Mussolini Urbanista: La Sventramento di Roma negli Anni del Consenso* (Rome, 1980); L. Barroera, *Via dei Fori Imperiali. La Zona Archeologica di Roma: Urbanistica, Beni Artistici e Politica Cultuale* (Venice, 1983); Maria Wyke, *Projecting the Past: Ancient Rome, Cinema and History* (New York and London, 1987); and Tim Benton, 'Rome Reclaims its Empire', in Dawn Ades *et al.*, eds., *Art and Power: Europe under the Dictators, 1930–1945* (London, 1995). The well-illustrated guide to the great model of Rome made under Mussolini in 1937 is on sale in various translations, including Leonardo dal Maso, *La Rome des Césars* (Florence, 1999).

On German interest in the Forum, see Albert Speer, *Inside the Third Reich* (London, 1970); Léon Krier, *Albert Speer,*

*Architecture 1932–42* (Brussels, 1985), which covers both Hitler and Mussolini; and Alexander Scobie, *Hitler's State Architecture: The Impact of Classical Antiquity* (University Park, PA and London, 1990). On Hitler's inspections of the antiquities of Rome and the archaeologist who guided him, see Marcello Barbanera, *Ranuccio Bianchi Bandinelli: Biografia ed Epistolario di un Grande Archeologo* (Milan, 2003).

The quotation on p. 220 about the use of memory in appreciating the rich, layered deposit of Roman remains in the neighbourhood of the Forum is from Sigmund Freud, *Civilisation and its Discontents*, trans., by David McLintock, (London, 2000).

The best monograph on any of the American architects who incorporated classical sources in the first forty years of the twentieth century is Steven Bedford, *John Russell Pope: Architect of Empire* (New York, 1998). On architects currently working in the classical tradition, see Robert Stern, *Modern Classicism* (London, 1988); *Allan Greenberg: Selected Works* (London, 1995); Léon Krier, *Architecture: Choice or Fate* (London, 1998); *Demetri Porphyrios Associates: Recent Work* (London, 1999); Richard John and David Watkin, *John Simpson: The Queen's Gallery, Buckingham Palace, and Other Works* (London, 2002); Richard John, *Thomas Gordon Smith: The Rebirth of Classical Architecture* (London, 2002); and David Watkin, *Radical Classicism: The Architecture of Quinlan Terry* (New York, 2006). The most recent commentaries and illustrations of Vitruvius are Ingrid Rowland and Thomas Noble Howe, *Vitruvius: Ten Books of Architecture* (Cambridge, 1999); and Thomas Gordon Smith, *Vitruvius on Architecture* (New York, 2003). The best modern translation, into French, is that by Pierre Gros, *et al* (Paris, 10 vols, 1969–2004).

# LIST OF ILLUSTRATIONS

from the east (restoration drawing by E.-G.
Coquart, 1863)
36. Map made in 1938 of Hitler's journey through
Rome (Christopher Woodward, *In Ruins*, Chatto &
Windus, 2001)

## PLAN

Plan of the Forum, based on Filippo Coaraelli, *Rome and
Environs: An Archaeological Guide* (University of California
Press, 2007), fig. 13, pp. 42–3. Re-drawn by Tom Cross

Endpapers: View from the centre of the Forum (Piranesi,
*Vedute di Roma, c.* 1748–78)

While every effort has been made to contact copyright
holders of illustrations, the author and publishers would be
grateful for information about any illustrations where they
have been unable to trace them, and would be glad to make
amendments in further editions.

# ACKNOWLEDGEMENTS

I am most grateful to Professor Mary Beard for going far beyond the call of duty as editor of this series in attempting to educate me in the world of ancient Rome and in making numerous rich suggestions for improving several successive versions of the text. The whole process has been most entertaining, especially our brief escape from term in Cambridge to stay in warm spring weather in the Hotel Forum in Rome, the ideal spot from which to survey the Forum. It is a pleasure to thank Peter Carson of Profile Books for his useful suggestions and for his important support for the reliance on Piranesi as a valuable guide.

I am also indebted to the Librarians of the Society of Antiquaries, the British School at Rome, and of the Faculties of Classics and of Architecture and History of Art in Cambridge. Further help has come from Dr Roman Roth and Dr Manolo Guerci in Cambridge, and from Professor Andrew Wallace-Hadrill and Robert Coates-Stephens, both of the British School at Rome.

# INDEX

Figures in italics indicate captions; main references are shown in bold type.

[ 256 ]

[ 264 ]

# WONDERS OF THE WORLD

This is a small series of books, under the general editorship of Mary Beard, that will focus on some of the world's most famous sites or monuments.